WESTONBIRT

Association News

2015

Westonbirt Association News 2015

Published in paperback and ebook by Hawkesbury Press 2015
Hawkesbury Upton, Gloucestershire, UK GL9 1AS
www.hawkesburypress.com

For further information about the Westonbirt Association,
please contact
Westonbirt School
Tetbury, Gloucestershire, UK, GL8 8QG
www.westonbirt.gloucs.sch.uk

ISBN 978-0-9930879-3-6
Also available as an ebook

British Library Cataloguing in Publication Data
A CiP catalogue record for this book is available from the British Library

Contents

Westonbirt Association Officers 2015

EXECUTIVE COMMITTEE

President Ms Karen Olsen
Honorary Secretary Mrs Leigh Ralphs
Honorary Treasurer Miss Louise Matley
News Finances and Distribution Mrs Jenny Webb
News Editor Mrs Debbie Young
Representative on the Governing Body
Mrs Karen Broomhead
Headmistress Mrs Natasha Dangerfield
Staff Representative Mrs Mary Phillips

Co-opted Members
Mrs Serena Jones
Mrs Sarah Clunie

Support Roles
Membership Assistant Mrs Jane Reid
PA to Headmistress Miss Abbie Cooke

GENERAL COMMITTEE

The Executive Committee and all the Section Representatives

2015 ANNUAL GENERAL MEETING

*To be held at Westonbirt School on Association Day,
Saturday 3 October 2015*

VICE PRESIDENTS
Mrs P Faust
Dr A Grocock
Mrs M Henderson
Mrs G Hylson-Smith
Miss M Newton
Mr H A Nickols

HONORARY MEMBERS
Mr R Baggs
Mrs E A Bullock
Miss V Byrom-Taylor
Miss D Challis
Mrs S Cole
Miss B D Cooper
Miss N O Davies
Mr P Dixon
Mrs D Elsdon
Mrs S English
Mrs L J Evans
Miss M Evett
Mrs M R Farley
Mrs J Hutchings
Mrs V A Innes
Mrs R J Kingston
Miss E M Miller
Miss P E Morris
Mrs H Nickols
Mrs H Owen
Miss O T Pasco
Mr D Philbey
Mrs H R Price
Mrs A M Reed
Mrs A Rodber
Mrs D Thombs
Mrs C Tilley
Miss S Urquhart
Mrs M Walding
Mrs L J Webb
Miss K S Yates
Mrs D Young

Editorial

From the retiring Editor

To my great relief (and maybe yours) Debbie Young has come to the rescue and has taken over as Editor of this News.

Debbie was working as Development Director at Westonbirt when I started as Editor 10 years ago and showed me the ropes of what was needed, so I know the News is in good hands. She is forward-thinking and not averse to change. I have a feeling she will bring us into the twenty-first century! Thank you, Debbie.

Mrs Serena Jones

From the new Editor

I always hold that no-one ever really leaves Westonbirt, whether staff or pupils, so it came as no surprise when I found myself volunteering to take over from Serena Jones as Editor of this important and always fascinating magazine. For the last decade, she has taken meticulous care of the News and the Westonbirt diaspora that it serves, and gently evolved it into its current state. She has handed over the baton to me with her characteristic kindness and attention to detail, and I wish her many years of enjoying the News as a reader.

For those of you who don't know who I am and are wondering which Section I'm from, I'm a former member of staff. I left in 2010, after spending 13 years writing, editing and producing the school's various publications, first in print and increasingly online as the internet age took hold. I was also on the Westonbirt Association Executive Committee for all 13 years, and some of my happiest memories of the school involve the alumni.

I left Westonbirt in order to write and self-publish books, and I've since gained a great deal of practical experience in the technology that allows authors to produce their own books to professional standards. I'm pleased to put my knowledge at the Association's disposal for the production of the News.

Gone are the days when you had to order a print run of a set number and hope you'd estimated correctly! In future, the News will be produced using print-on-demand technology, which means that we will be able to print any quantity as and when required, even a single copy. The Association will continue to order a substantial stock to distribute to members who have paid a subscription. Alternatively, you may order a copy online from Amazon, wherever you are in the world. Each copy will be produced and despatched from your local Amazon depot, saving postage and reducing the impact on the environment, compared to mass despatch from the UK, where postage costs continue to soar. You will also be able to order it from other online retailers such as Foyles and Waterstones, and from all good high street bookshops by quoting ISBN number 978-0993087974.

In addition, we will make the News available as an ebook, adding appeal to younger members, for whom reading on electronic devices is second nature. It will be available not only from Amazon but also from other leading suppliers of ebooks such as Kobo, Nook and iBooks. This will also save production and distribution costs.

As you can see, although the Westonbirt Association is rooted in its proud and historic heritage, it is keeping up with the times and looking towards its future.

I have very much enjoyed compiling this issue, and I am, as ever, astonished and impressed by the achievements, activities and interests reported by Association members down the generations. It is a pleasure to help celebrate them in the pages of this magazine.

Mrs Debbie Young

President's Report

This edition of our Association News is being published for the first time online, so some of you may have ordered your copy from the internet. When the Association was founded in 1930 it was to enable those first leavers to keep in touch with each other and the school. The formation then of an "old girls' club" became the forerunner of the Association that we have today. Our aim, in keeping in touch, was to set up year groups, or sections, with representatives that would look after their contemporaries, gathering news and information over the years, to compile firstly into an annual magazine, the Association News, and then address details which we formed into a record of all our members.

The Association handed over details of its members to the school in 2000, together with some funds to set up a database bringing together membership details which the school had not previously kept. This database has been upgraded in recent years and now contains both address and career details of many of our members. Both the Association and the school use the database to keep in touch with members and to inform them of the many events that they can take part in. As well as the database, in striving to stay in touch in the twenty-first century, the Westonbirt Association is now on Facebook, LinkedIn and Twitter, so do take a look for yourselves.

We are an excellent source of careers advice for the school. Since last October two stimulating careers days were run where former pupils returned to talk about their careers and to showcase their own businesses. It is so inspiring to sixth formers to see former pupils talking about their lives in the workplace.

We have raised money over the years through our Memorial Bursary, in memory of five former pupils who died during World War II, in service to their country. This bursary has enabled many past and current girls to start, continue or finish their education at Westonbirt.

We also have a small Modern Languages Travel Award, in recognition of Mary Henderson's time as Head at Westonbirt, to raise money for a girl each year to travel in Europe. We have in recent years taken part in two telethons, organised by the school, to raise money firstly for the Marriott Music Centre and more recently for the Skills4Life Project.

The Association today has captured a wider audience by arranging several trips and events. These include two trips to the Gardens at Highgrove House, a visit to the House of Lords, and for those members that were at school during the war a special visit to Bowood House, to which they had been evacuated. The school helps us with many events and invited us to a carol service in London last December, which was so popular that another is planned for this year.

On Saturday 3 October 2015, we will be celebrating our 85th birthday, at Westonbirt. The day will include a church service, lunch and a lacrosse match. We do hope many of you will join us.

I hope you enjoy reading this year's News, however it comes to you. We very much appreciate the help of Debbie Young, one of our Honorary members, who has taken over as Editor and implemented the production online so that members will be able to order a copy anywhere in the world to be delivered to their home.

Ms Karen Olsen

Headmistress's Report

Dear Association Members

Once again we are at a point of no return and the school has settled into the rhythm of public exams that have us in their grip for at least nine weeks of this Summer Term.

The girls are all in good spirits, so much so that I have had to come down rather hard on high-spirited high jinks that are also known as pranks. It seems to be a traditional event. I wonder as I write this Association Report for 2015, how many of you may have been involved in such antics over the years? I am confident, that, as ever, there would be some interesting stories amongst you!

It has been wonderful to have seen a number of old girls this year. We were delighted with the success of our first Association Carol Service in London, and we hope that with such a firm foundation below us, that we will repeat the event with as much festive sparkle this year. On Saturday 5th December, we will be holding our next service at All Saints Church in Fulham, London. It is a traditional service in many ways but we are fortunate to be able to bring the Chamber Choir with us and hope therefore that you may be tempted to join us. If that is not enough, families are more than welcome and we will ensure there are enough mince pies to go round.

We have also been delighted to welcome back a wide variety of you who have generously given your time for an Inspiring Women's Day and other talks and lectures. We consider it vital that current girls are given as many opportunities to understand what careers are available to them and the paths that they can take to get there when they leave. We are extremely grateful for the inspiration that these sessions bring and hope that we can continue to develop this.

It was a delight to meet some of you at School before the Highgrove Garden Tour, and I am pleased you enjoyed a dry day, as well as a look around the school on your return. I was amused to hear that many of your secret areas for stashing treats are still accessible within wardrobes and behind doors, and that you were pleased to see updated furniture and carpets in the dorms! Talks of swimming in the cellars however are entirely unwelcome as they still carry considerable 'cool' credibility and as you can imagine in the age of compliance, are an absolute no-no!

As a school, we continue to pack a significant amount in to the relatively short days. We have been experiencing great success in Drama, Music and Sport. These areas are steadily developing with a good deal of energy and we hope this continues. There is always an event to be taken in. Please know that these are as much open to our old girls as to parents and students in our current cohort. The subject departments continue to keep pace with academic reform; we are of course fortunate to be able to continue to deliver strong and consistent teaching in environments I know many of you remember well. Technological development sees every child with an iPad as part of their necessary equipment, which has created quite a change in both the look and feel of lessons. However, that important balance between technology and sound teaching remains, and while we continue to look forward, we know what works well in the classroom.

The fabric of the building has remained unchanged this year, but investment has gone into the much-required overhaul of the IT systems to ensure there is sufficient internet bandwidth for the new demands to work seamlessly. Holford did not design this beautiful building with such intricacies in mind, so you can imagine this has not been entirely smooth sailing. The gardens continue to delight and we have worked hard to create some better vistas, as would have been the original intent. Through the summer we are open twice a week, so please feel able to visit then, although you are of course welcome to arrange a visit any weekday through my PA, Abbie Cooke.

As I finish this on a lovely evening, the Sixth Form are busy preparing for the Leavers' Ball with a rather on-trend Oscars theme, including a red carpet which runs down the centre of the Great Hall! The next steps for the girls are as wide-ranging as ever and include a number of Art, Academic and Business degrees to destinations ranging from Glasgow and Durham to Ohio and Florida and, once again, Association numbers will swell, and the cycle of the school continues.

With my best wishes
Mrs Natasha Dangerfield

Westonbirt Association Carol Service Report

On Saturday 13 December 2014, Westonbirt School journeyed to London to connect with our community of former pupils. Over 40 old girls and their families joined the Headmistress and Association for a traditional Westonbirt Carol Service at St Dionis Church in Parsons Green. The service was hosted by the Association and led by School Chaplain, Reverend Alice Monaghan, with music by the Chamber Choir.

It was a crisp, sunny day and we were thrilled to welcome so many people into the warmth of the Church, where past and present pupils and staff joined together to sing traditional carols. Our Chamber Choir and Flute Quartet very generously gave their time just a day in to the Christmas holidays, providing accompaniment and delighting the audience with their festive tunes.

All enjoyed delicious mulled wine and mince pies whilst looking at archive photos and reminiscing about their times at the school, as well as learning about the school in the present day. It was a wonderful opportunity for us to connect with former pupils and hear about their lives since leaving Westonbirt.

This year the event will be held on Saturday 5 December 2015 at All Saints Church, Pryors Bank, Bishop's Avenue, Fulham, London SW6 3LA. Why not gather together your peers and come to celebrate and reminisce? You could even form your own choir!

Miss Abbie Cooke

Careers Events Supported by Association Members

Support from former pupils has contributed to making it a great school year in the Information, Advice and Guidance Centre (formerly the Careers Department).

October saw "Enterprising Futures" with brilliant input from **Sallie Bale**, **Nancy Lawson (White)**, **Chantal Michelin (Lane)**, **Lorraine Stanton (Marin)** and **Rebecca Williams**. They each described their varied businesses to pupils in Years 10-13, as well as to pupils from neighbouring schools.

January gave rise to "Inspiring Women" with marvellous talks from seven former pupils: **Charlotte Boyes**, **Claire Galer (Dorman)**, **Cordelia Gover (Harries)**, **Hermione Harbutt (Berry)**, **Georgina Lee**, **Natasha Seel**, and **Jo Wilkie**. The sixth form were truly inspired.

In June, "What Lies Ahead for School Leavers" was held for the Year 12 pupils and included a talk by **Alice Coleman** about her post A Level route as an apprentice, and how it helped launch her career in marketing.

It was a great thrill to meet again with these young women. My grateful thanks goes to them all for giving up their valuable time to support current pupils. I would also like to thank former pupil **Karen Olsen** for her continued support at these events.

Do please let me know if you would like to share your experiences since leaving school with current pupils and pass on helpful hints and tips about skills for life as well as career backgrounds. I am now looking for volunteers for the next "Inspiring Women" event on Friday 29 January 2016, and I can be contacted through the School on 01666 881332 and by email to *adunn@westonbirt.org*.

Mrs Ann Dunn

Deaths Notified Since 2014

Name	Section	Died
Doritie Kettlewell	1	29/8/14
Joan Clydesmuir (Booth)	6	9/7/14
June Gardner-Brown (Napier)	7	18/7/12
Elizabeth Massey (Merry)	8	30/11/13
Rosemary Claire Porter-Waters (Porter)	contemporary of 9	15/9/14
Marta Inskip	contemporary of 10	9/5/14
Nancy Burnett (Elizabeth Clark-Turner)	13	26/7/14
Daphne Wells (Touche)	14	5/1/15
Prudence Molnar (Wurtzberg)	contemporary of 14	5/11/13
Mary Prentice (Porter)	contemporary of 14	1/1/04
Joan Freeland (Temple)	15	3/12/14
Penny Nairne (Penelope Chauncy Bridges)	15	23/12/14
Elizabeth Ross (Brigg)	16	16/12/14
Ruth von Ledebur (Niemann)	18	26/6/14
Rosemary Wurtzberg	contemporary of 18/19	c 2008
Paddy Scott-Clark (Patricia Angus)	25	18/10/14
Margaret Niewland (Alexander)	27	29/12/14
Sue Powell (Watkins)	27	30/9/14
Juliet Townsend (Smith)	29	29/11/14
Anne Bament (Best)	30	12/14
Charmian Reeve (Rooper)	contemporary of 32/33	18/12/14
Helen Danielsen (Davies)	33	24/10/14
Miss Barbara Scatchard	ex-staff	2001
Miss Celia Graham	ex-staff	4/11/14

Obituaries

Miss Doritie Kettlewell
(29 February 1916 - 29 August 2014)

Doritie Kettlewell, the youngest of six children, was one of the first pupils at Westonbirt, having previously had a governess. She was listed in the May 1928 address list as Sheila Doritie Ellen Kettlewell; to school friends she was known as Squib. Considered at school to be a good writer, her real passion was art. Sylvia Martin (Spice) of Section 3 remembers their sitting together at the back of the Latin class, drawing.

After Westonbirt, Doritie studied at the Slade, and Sylvia at the Royal College of Music. For some of this time, they shared digs in Kensington; Sylvia remembers Doritie as having, rather than ambition, an overwhelming desire to paint and draw. Doritie was not a natural early riser; Sylvia was, and often had to smuggle her breakfast up to their room and eat it very quietly. In an attempt to liven up the bathroom, Doritie painted cherubs over the walls; the landlady said that they should be removed, immediately!

When the war came, Doritie joined the WAAF. Working as a wireless operator, she frequently had the distressing experience of listening to pilots as they dealt with crippled aircraft. Her tendency to absent-mindedness resulted not only in her stockings being often laddered and wrinkled at the ankles, but also to her leaving the call signs for Bomber Command on the London Underground.

After the war, she went back to art. She took private commissions; she also taught at GLC evening classes, at Hornsey School of Art, and at the London School of Fashion – she had an abiding interest in textiles and the history of fashion. She toured America with Sylvia, and was part of a small team that took a Trade and Industry exhibition, "British Fashions through the Ages", around Japan.

After further training at the Central School of Art, Doritie joined her brother Jasper and his wife, working with stained glass, before buying a house with a garden in north London, in De Beauvoir Town, where she built a workshop to house her glass kiln. Her basement lodger of the 1970s remembers working there with turned wood and metal, while Doritie worked on stained glass, fused glass, paintings of wild flowers and illustrations for books. He commented that she was not at all absent-minded when using the kiln, checking progress frequently though the spy hole.

It was during this period that she designed and created the stained glass given to Westonbirt in commemoration and thanks by pupils from the first five years. The original intention had been for a window in what was then the parish church, but the necessary faculty could not be obtained; conveniently, the hall in the Orangery was about to be constructed, with north-facing windows that would enable the work to be seen to advantage. Doritie's work appears in other churches, in particular a 20 foot high glass icon of Christ as High Priest at St George and All Saints, Tufnell Park.

Her garden gave her great joy and fulfilment, as did the village-like atmosphere of De Beauvoir Town; she was important in the founding of the De Beauvoir Garden Club. In her late 80s, she moved to her nephew's care home in Devon, which she described as like a long house party. When Sylvia visited her there, she would find her the "life and soul of the party [...] a lively and loving companion and abiding friend."

Jane Reid

Miss Celia Graham
(1ˢᵗ March 1955 - 4ᵗʰ November 2014)

Celia Graham was a Westonbirt girl through and through. She loved the school and the place; the environment suited her and as a member of staff for 28 years, 18 of them as Head of PE, she was a part of the stonework. She was hugely respected in the staff room for her commitment to the girls, to the PE and later Learning Support departments, and for the high standards she set. She was an excellent organiser and a wise boss, appreciative of her colleagues and generous with her praise. She was also a highly competitive and skilful teacher, doing her best with the girls she had and, especially in lacrosse, giving larger schools a run for their money, regularly having players selected for the West of England team and, in the case of Michelle Lawson, for England.

In 2002 Celia decided to stand down as Head of PE. She then retrained very successfully in Learning Support, developing strong relationships with the girls she taught one-to-one and finding the new chapter in her career particularly rewarding. She was throughout an excellent class tutor, giving her girls both the considered advice they sought and the boundaries they needed.

Celia was a strong and inspirational teacher; she was also a great colleague, always supportive and never afraid to speak her mind. She was fun and spirited and had the gift of friendship in abundance. She was fiercely loyal to her friends and always thoughtful and generous as well as tolerant and accepting. As in the staff room, she called a spade a spade, knowing how to say difficult things which needed to be said, but always in a kind way.

Celia was a talented all round sportswoman. Outside school she was an active golf and tennis club member, and she loved to ride her horses, Stilton and later Bentley, with the Berkeley Hunt on Wednesdays, her day off. She was devoted to her family, and also to her dogs, Scrumpy Jack and then Bonnie, who were both very much part of the Westonbirt community.

Celia retired in 2012 in order to pursue her many interests and to spend more time with her partner, Ian. Sadly this was not to be, and her cancer finally caught up with her on November 4th 2014. The packed chapel for her thanksgiving service in January was testament to the very high esteem in which she was held by every generation of pupils she taught, as well as by her many friends and colleagues throughout her life. We gave thanks for Celia's full and loving life and prayed that her legacy would continue through us as we, in the words of David Harkins's poem read at her funeral, would "do what she would want: smile, open our eyes, love and go on".

Mrs Mary Henderson

SECTION NEWS

Thank You to Section Representatives
The Association is enormously grateful for the hard work and attention to detail shown each year by the Section Representatives, who volunteer to collect and collate the news from their former classmates. Modern technology makes this much easier than years ago, with many of even the most senior members sending in their news by email.

Thank You to Section Members
We are always pleased to hear members' news, so if you're a regular respondent, thank you very much for continuing to keep us posted.

If you've not sent in your own news for a while, please don't hold back. Even if you feel you have nothing to report, we still like to know that you are alive and well, and that we have the right contact details for you. We also love hearing reminiscences about your own time at Westonbirt.

Youngest Sections First
This year, we're continuing the practice of starting with news from the most recent leavers. In the early, heady days of their higher education and careers, reporting back to their *alma mater* may not be top of their list of priorities, so their news is often brief, but still interesting to read.

There seems to be a correlation between the length of absence from Westonbirt and the length of a member's news report, not least because many older members give a thorough round-up of their children, grandchildren and even great-grandchildren!

In all sections, we have listed members in alphabetical order by their current surname, to make it easier to find your friends.

If reading any of their news makes you hanker after a nostalgic trip back to Westonbirt, we'd love to see you at our next Reunion Day (Saturday 3 October 2015), and the school also welcomes visits by appointment all year round. To arrange to visit, or for any information regarding the Association, such as the current contact details for your Section Rep, please do not hesitate to contact Miss Abbie Cooke, PA to the Headmistress, via her school email address, acooke@westonbirt.org, or by telephoning her on 01666 880333.

Staff Section

Section Representative:
Miss Diana Challis

Mrs Betty Bullock With constantly deteriorating eyesight and hearing, I feel frustrated at all that I can't do now I am 95 years old, but I really feel blessed with a loving family and friends, able to stay in my granny flat here, in a pleasant village with so many kind friends and neighbours and a really good situation. Best wishes to anyone who might remember me from Westonbirt 1967-1977.

Miss Valerie Byrom-Taylor After a very happy reunion at my home in July 2013 I have been pleased to meet up again with several schoolfriends who came. In particular **Anne Millman**, **Jenefer Greenwood** and **Alison Dorey** have met each other since, and I was delighted to be invited to tea at Anne Millman's when the others were there. It was a pleasure to see Mrs Millman too and look at photographs of her trip to Antarctica where she went to celebrate her 90th birthday!

Miss Diana Challis I keep as busy as ever in Tetbury and frequently guide parties around Westonbirt House. Last year saw me travelling to Skye in May, when the weather was such that it could have been a Mediterranean island! Later I visited friends in the Lake District, and in August I went with the City of London Historical Society to Belgium on a tour of the First World War battlefields. We stayed in Ypres and it was a very moving experience, especially the daily ceremony at the Menin Gate. Later I went with our local Trefoil Guild to Switzerland. We had a marvellous time in the mountains and were able to take the railway up the Jungfraugoch.

Mrs Susan Cole 2014 was for me rather dominated by having to accompany other people to hospital appointments, but fortunately, I have remained well! I enjoyed the hot summer on the golf course, and did manage to improve my game a bit. The good news for the year was the birth of my great-nephew in May. He is a delight! I was able to fit in visits to friends, and had holidays in the Wye Valley, France and Amsterdam. I've kept in touch with many former colleagues and pupils, which is always nice. I still miss **Celia Graham**, it seems so unfair that she has gone. She was such a brave lady.

Mrs Mary Rose Farley (Bateman) My news isn't really about me – am I vegetating? But this winter I have been visiting **Miss N O Davies** (erstwhile Holford Housemistress) who had been in hospital for a long time but is thankfully home at last. She is much older than me (same age as the Queen) but we have been friends ever since the 1950s at Westonbirt.

Mrs Mary Henderson We are enjoying life in Bath, and I continue to build up a portfolio of educational, musical and sporting activities. I am now a fully-fledged Blue Badge tourist guide for the South West region and am qualified to guide in both English and French. Future bookings include walking tours of Bath for French school parties and tour manager for Bath Choral Society's trip to Paris and Chartres in July. In January we greatly enjoyed returning to Westonbirt for the Winter Wonderland Ball. I am currently vice-captain of the ladies' section of Westonbirt golf club and a board member of Westonbirt Leisure. I still wonder how I had time to work!

Mrs Jill Hutchings There is nothing earth-shattering to report from my peaceful retired life, for which I am very grateful! It is quite clear that the world of teaching has become a foreign place, full of modern equipment which I am happy not to have to master. My only real contact with the classroom is through my grandchildren, one of whom will be taking A Levels this year, and the other will be tackling GCSEs. The 18 year old has not hitherto been known for his dedication to academic work, but the prospect of applying to university has focused his mind somewhat, and he might yet surprise me.

My lack of ambition when it comes to travel was well indicated after Christmas when members of the family variously departed for New York and Marrakesh, and I was mightily relieved to be going no further than London for a short burst of metropolitan life. Much more to my liking was our first experience of a river cruise when we went from Budapest to Nuremburg.

This year, to celebrate a rather significant birthday, we are having a holiday with the rest of the family in France, actually in the small town where Richard I was fatally shot by a sniper. I hope to avoid such a dramatic fate.

Mrs Gillian Hylson-Smith I am well and happy in Bath and very blessed to be in good health – so far! I am not without seeing ex-Westonbirt staff as **Mary Henderson**, **Mary Young** and **Sue Montgomery** all live in Bath, and we often bump into each other. It was very sad to be at **Celia Graham**'s memorial service. She was such a good teacher and Head of Department. My husband and his twin brother will be 80 in June (*deo volente*, for those of you who remember any Latin!) so we are planning celebrations in London. *Tempus* really does *fugit* so *carpe diem* etc. Love to all.

Miss Margo Miller The march of suburbia, converging upon our sanctuary of pastoral living as the mayor and council pursue their relentless design of "making Auckland the most liveable city in the world", is bringing more and more horse people in search of grazing. We now have the pleasure of welcoming the owner of a beautiful Anglo-Arab mare (nice dog too!) who comes for lessons and practice in classical dressage from Sue, who after many years of retirement is enjoying the re-use of her lifelong commitment to this ideal.

Mrs Helen Price I am now really retired, as I have stopped teaching dyslexic students at HMP Bristol. That gives me more time for playing my bassoon, tennis when the weather allows, and learning Spanish. I'm still very involved in Sherston Church and continue my Guiding with Trefoil Guild. There's always a lot to do in Tetbury: walking group, film club and theatre group. Luckily my husband and I are still fit, so we can enjoy holidays in Europe – this year Sicily, a river cruise on the Elbe, a quick trip to Germany to visit a friend and Spain in October.

Mrs Diana Thombs I'm happy to answer **Miss Challis**'s appeal for news this year because I do, at last, have something exciting to report. At the ages of 75 and 76, Tony and I are at last to become grandparents at the end of March. This means, *dv*, that we should be celebrating his 21st when in our late 90s. Most friends of my age have celebrated 18th and 21st birthdays of grandchildren during the last decade, but I don't mean to grumble! I have asked to be in charge of his literary education, poor little mite. Otherwise, one new knee, working well, and the prospect of a second new one later this year.

I keep in regular contact with quite a few former colleagues, and recently had a very enjoyable lunch with **Clare Ryder Richardson**, now mother of two delightful girls and teaching in Malmesbury. She gave me news of many in her year, It's encouraging to see how many keep in contact even 20 and more years later.

The book club I belong to prospers well, and continues to widen my horizons, as do the Malmesbury and Cirencester NADFAS groups.

Miss Sheila Urquhart Another busy year enjoying retirement. I had a lovely visit to the Westonbirt area late September and managed to catch up with many friends. The school was looking splendid. Just about to go off to Iceland for two weeks with two different schools doing geography fieldwork. It is always lovely to hear from former pupils.

Mrs Debbie Young Somehow I found myself volunteering for the role of Editor of this magazine at the last Association AGM. How did that happen?! Actually, I'm glad to put my self-publishing skills and experience to good use for the Association. Having left Westonbirt in 2010 with the ambition to write books, I currently have five paperbacks to my name, plus a handful of ebook "singles". Two of the books, *Quick Change* and *Stocking Fillers*, are humorous short fiction, two are marketing guidebooks for authors, and the other is a fundraiser for diabetes charity JDRF. You can find out more about my books at my author website: *www.authordebbieyoung.com*.

When I'm not writing books, I work part-time as Commissioning Editor of the Alliance of Independent Authors' advice blog, networking with writers all over the world. I also provide marketing consultancy to individual authors.

I have just set up and run the first ever Hawkesbury Upton Literature Festival (*www.hulitfest.com*), featuring more than 20 authors, and that's now set to be an annual event. In my spare time (!) I help run the village youth club and am in increasing demand as a public speaker, either talking about writing and self-publishing at literary festivals and universities, or raising funds and awareness for the JDRF.

NEWS FROM SECTION MEMBERS

Section 83 (2014)
Section representative:
Amelie Sievers

Amelie Sievers has recently become a member and has kindly agreed to become the Section Rep for Section 83. Amelie joined Westonbirt for the Sixth Form and on completing her education rejoined the Sixth Form as Assistant Housemistress. She is now home in Germany to attend university. We look forward to news from Section 83 in the next edition.

Victoria Adams
Janine Bauer
Tara Clayton
Jennifer Craven
Georgina Fenn
Ella Kalfayan
Annabel Kimber
Bastienne Korts
Shirley Liao
Lucy Liu
Lara Macdonald
Charlotte McCulloch
Marta Navarro Urosa
Karen Ngan
Katie O'Neill
Mollie O'Neill
Caroline Oliver
Tertia Rollason
Amelia Schiller
Charlotte Strong
Luana Tanir
Natasha Tayler
Molly Turner
Anastasia Walsh
Angela Wang
Alice Wordsworth

Section 82 (2013)

Section representative:
Abi Lowes

Aisha Gross I am currently in my first year at Bournemouth University studying Tourism Management. Also playing lacrosse for the university 1st team.

Abigail Lowes This year I am working at Westonbirt as an Assistant Housemistress in Dorchester and am absolutely loving it. I am planning on just doing a year and then in July I am going to Canada to visit family before coming home to start my next adventure.

Lydia Marshall I am currently in my first year at Birmingham studying Drama and Theatre Studies. I am really enjoying it and can't wait for my second year.

Georgie Mobbs In my second year at Bristol UWE doing Business and Management, still enjoying it. Looking forward to only one more year to go until I graduate. I still keep in touch with a few of our year, but haven't seen as many as I would have liked due to uni. Hopefully will see some of you soon!

Fiona Vincent I am now in my second year at the University of Southampton studying medicine. I am still loving university life and trying to fit everything in. I am going travelling this summer with some university friends to make the most of the long summer holiday.

Issy Yerburgh I'm currently in my second year of Bristol Medical School, and hoping to spend an intercalated year studying for a BSc in either Physiology or Neuroscience.

Section 81 (2012)

Section representative:
Olivia Birkin-Hewitt
No news from Section 81 this year -
let's hope for a bumper update in the next edition!

Section 80 (2011)

Section representative:
Emily Clare

Sabrina Bertie I did a winter season as a host in St Anton, Austria and am now working as a supervisor in Waitrose. I am looking forward to the future, pursuing a career in travel and will hopefully move to London this year/early next year.

Emma Blackshire I graduated from the University of Reading last summer and then went travelling round South East Asia for two months. I am currently working for Fiat Chrysler Automobiles in their procurement department and working towards my Chartered Institute of Procurement and Supply qualification.

Sophie Cattermole I am currently living in Bristol and doing a Master's in history at the University of Bristol, and volunteer at the SS Great Britain.

Kiki Chiu I'm doing a product design course at Central Saint Martin's, graduating this year.

Emily Clare I graduated from Birmingham and went into property and surveying recruitment in central London. After a few months. I decided I should go into property myself and joined Foxtons Estate Agents as a lettings negotiator, which is awesome. I'm still living with Dave in Kingston.

Helena Cox I'm currently studying for a Masters in History of Art at Edinburgh University. At the moment I'm studying at the Sorbonne in Paris.

Amy Fletcher After graduating with a BA in Fine Art at Chelsea, I have secured a full-time position as studio project manager for global photographer Sam Robinson.

Tiva Gross I am currently at Oxford Brookes University studying sports coaching and physical education in my final year, then looking at doing a Masters in Cape Town.

Cordelia Hawkins I graduated from the University of the Arts, London last summer with a degree in Publishing. I am now working with a Fashion and Arts start-up in London where I am doing some fashion journalism, creating content for the website. I am also doing some temp work through Knightsbridge Recruitment to get more experience.

Rebekah Heaney I'm currently living in Dubai and working as a technical writer, saving up enough money to go back to University to do an MA.

Georgiana Hone I'm currently working for a private equity firm called Advent International as an Executive Assistant in London. I graduated from Aberystwyth University last summer with a degree in Art History, and before Christmas I was doing a business acumen course called Quest Professional.

Rosie Ingram I'm currently on a year-long industrial placement as a Food Technologist for a prawn manufacturer in Wiltshire. Then in September I'll be back at university to finish my degree, then hopefully find a job as a technologist or go into new product development.

Aungkana Jitsakul I'm currently studying in my final year of a Hotel Management (BSc and BBA) degree at Les Roches International School of Hotel Management in Switzerland.

Georgina Lee I am living in London and have been in my job now for nearly a year. I'm working for a company called Ocubis, the founder is Jon Hunt who also founded Foxtons Estate Agents. The building I work in is called Riverbank House, which is part of the Fulham Green complex in Putney.

Harriet Lewis I graduated from City University in sociology this year and am actually in Mexico at the moment and leaving here to start a two-month road trip in the USA, then to South America. When I get back to London, I'm hoping to continue training as a chef.

Georgina McCulloch I'm working for the Conservative party in the run up to this year's General Election.

Alicia Motley I'm doing my Masters in Digital Media Production at Oxford Brookes, and I'm Vice-President of the Lacrosse Team.

Caroline Railston-Brown I graduated last summer and am a sustainability consultant, working and soon to be living in Bristol.

Sioned Snowden I am back at uni carrying on with zoology after a year off volunteering for the Wiltshire Wildlife Trust. Hopefully plan to do vet medicine or medicine after graduating.

Chawadee Sriprasert I graduated from Imperial College London last summer with a degree in Biochemistry (BSc). I'm now a first year medical student studying at Thammasart University, Thailand.

Alice Steel I graduated last summer from Plymouth University with a degree in psychology, and I'm currently living in Plymouth and training to be a counsellor.

Felicity Welch I'm living in Upton-upon-Severn and work as a Veterinary Nurse in a large equine referral practice after getting my degree in Equine Business Management last year.

Ashley White In my final year at Oxford doing PPE currently. Life is thus very dull. Was in the boat race squad but I quit to focus on my finals last month.

Georgina Ziff I'm doing my final year in psychology at Manchester Metropolitan then hopefully will do a year's work experience as an assistant psychologist, and then do my PhD in clinical psychology MHA.

Section 79 (2010)
Section representative:
Sophie Martin

Charlotte Hunt Charlotte is now in her fifth year of medical school, and will be graduating in four months' time. She has her first job as a foundation doctor starting in July, in Wales.

Jess Kruger and Clementine Sharland Jess and Clemmie are currently travelling around South America together for a sixth-month period.

Grace Lee Grace has graduated from her MA in English Literature and is now working as a Teaching Assistant for Year 2. She hopes to start a primary PGCE this September. She has also just achieved permanent residency in England.

Sophie Martin Sophie is due to leave for two months' voluntary work in Canada on the 7th April, where she will be working on farms helping to look after animals such as alpacas, horses, peacocks and parrots.

Section 78 (2009)

Section representative:
Amy Falkenburg

Amy Falkenburg Emails or letters were sent to everyone for whom we have contact details, but no news was sent in. As for news of myself, having left the University of Exeter nearly two years ago, where I studied English Literature, I now live in Islington in London, and I've since worked for Red Bull, hopping around various departments within the business. From working for their Spinal Cord Injury Research Foundation Wings For Life, I am now coming to an end of a 12 month internship with their Formula One Team, Red Bull Racing, where I work in the fast-paced marketing team. Who knows what next... I'm looking to stick within the business or move to another awe-inspiring brand with a similar culture and ethos. Any ideas/suggestions on hot jobs from alumni are always welcome!

Section 77 (2008)

Section representative:
Portia Ingram

Kimberly Evans Kim did a BA degree in International Business with French at the Royal Agricultural College, Cirencester. She then did her primary PGCE at Oxford Brookes. She has become a primary school teacher in Highworth and is PE Coordinator for the school.

Portia Ingram Portia is living in Guildford, Surrey and has recently moved with Matthew, her boyfriend of six years, to a new house which they're busy decorating. She's currently working at a marketing agency called OgilvyOne dnx and loves it. She really enjoys being the section rep for her year and being able to keep in touch with all the girls.

Elizabeth Kennet (Hoaksey) Liz was married to Jonathon Kennett on the 16th August 2014. They had a wonderful day surrounded by friends and family, and she now lives with him not far from Oxford. Working for a luxury travel company, she still volunteers with the museums industry as often as possible as a historical textile advisor.

Lucy Matthews (Clare) After becoming Lucy Matthews in June 2014, Lucy is delighted to announce that baby Ben Matthews was born on 22nd February! She is now well and truly settled in Cardiff with her husband, two-year-old daughter Amelia and newborn son. She is just about to finish the second year of her degree in Child Psychology and Education at USW with hopes of becoming a primary school teacher.

Natasha Seel Tash is currently undertaking her final law exams on the Legal Practice Course at BPP Law School in London. She (finally!) starts her job as a trainee solicitor at Watson Farley and Williams in August this year. She will have two months in between studying and starting at the firm so is planning a trip to South America this summer.

Lottie Sharland Lottie is currently living in central London with friends from university. She works for the same branding agency, Curious, that she has been at for the past two years but has changed roles, moving from Project Management to Brand Strategy, which she starts at the beginning of May. She still see lots of friends from Westonbirt and went out to Australia in November to visit **Rosie Margesson** and **Tessa Moreland** while they were travelling, before Rosie made the move back to England, where she's now staying in Lottie's spare room!

Section 76 (2007)
Section representative:
new representative needed
Please contact Leigh Ralphs via the School if you'd like to volunteer.
*Consequently there is no news from Section 76 this year -
let's hope for a bumper update in the next edition!*

Section 75 (2006)
Section representative:
Charlotte Boyes

Anna Baker Working as a qualified teacher in Banbury, teaching Food Technology.

Charlotte Boyes Veterinary surgeon near Burford, working towards a post-graduate business certificate.

Sarah Butler FI and multi-corporate account manager for a global and commercial investment bank in Singapore.

Jeni Chan Associate at an investment bank in Singapore.

Hannah Cunild Marketing manager living in Bristol.

Amelia Davies Working in London as a recruiter.

Elle Ewan Teaching A level Psychology in Winchester. Had a beautiful baby girl called Annabelle on the 14th June 2014.

Sophie Fane Working in London at a primary school, teaching Year 3 boys.

Sawako Fukui Qualified F2 doctor working in Tokyo.

Sarah Goretzki Working in Paediatrics (neonatal care).

Wendy Hagues (Browne) Working as a researcher at Cambridge University having just completed her PhD. Got married in July 2014 at Westonbirt School to Edward Hagues.

Camilla Jenkin Working in travel PR in London.

Pam Moth Living in London and embarking on developing an online business.

Lois Slater Working as an estate agent in Dorset and studying for an MNAEA.

Haruka Sakurai Working at a tax firm in Tokyo.

Elaine Tsui Working as an architect in London.

Rosalind Wade Working and living in Germany as a nanny and English teacher. Speaking German.

Emma Logan Accountancy manager for a training consultancy in London.

Margaret Shum Land administrator in the Hong Kong government.

Section 74 (2005)
Section representative:
New representative needed

Rebecca Massey Rebecca has resigned as Section Representative. Her section and the Association would like to thank her for her hard work as the first section 74 representative. If anyone would like to volunteer to replace her, please contact Leigh Ralphs, the Association Secretary, who will be very pleased to hear from you!

Section 73 (2004)
Section representative:
Emily Stephenson

Suzie Drewett Since the last news update, Suzie has moved from Bath to London. She now lives in Surbiton and works as a property manager for Robert Irving Burns, just off Oxford Street, managing commercial and residential properties for clients in the West End. She is currently training for a cycle ride from London to Gibraltar in September with a friend for the charity Beat.

Hannah Knowles (Ewan) After the birth of her daughter, Freya, in December, Hannah is having a wonderful time getting to know her. She will keep writing, but plans to take some time to explore a new career path. This will continue to be in the field of food education, but for now she's got her hands full!

Letitia Mckie Letitia now has a new job as a learning officer for Fulham Palace. She also wrote and performed her first stand-up poetry show last year at a theatre in East London.

Emily Stephenson Emily continues to work at cazenove+loyd in the Latin America team and has been there nearly five years. In October last year she got engaged and is very much looking forward to getting married at home in July, with Robin Baggs on the organ and Philip Dixon taking the service!

Saskya Vandoorne Saskya is back living in New York, working as an editorial producer on CNN International's flagship business program Quest Means Business.

Section 72 (2003)

Section representative:
Carey Logan

Carey Logan Very well and happy living in Malmesbury and working in Cancer Trials in Bath Hospital. Saw **Fiona Tubbs** a month ago who is working as a solicitor.

Florence Warrington I am getting married this year on 25th June. I have also been made permanent in my job (finally!) in A & E of Cavan General Hospital, Ireland.

Section 71 (2002)

Section representative:
Joanna Colson

Narisa Cherdjareewatananun I'm still living in Singapore. It's been almost 9 years now. I'm working in branding and visual merchandising for a furniture brand called Christopher Guy. I'm also freelancing as interior stylist. If anyone needs their house done, let me know!

Joanna Colson Working for the same family now to 10 years as a PA/Nanny. Living in Gloucestershire. Hoping to get a WB get-together planned over the next few months.

Lucinda Dalton Living in London and working for a bespoke matchmaking service.

Hattie Fisher I work for the NHS at Maudsley as an executive PA. Hope all are well!

Alice Lycett Green I'm living in London and still working for Sentebale, a children's charity operating in Lesotho in SA, looking after the marketing and communications.

Hannah Lynn Still living in Kl, gave up work last year to write novels. Plan was somewhat interrupted by the arrival of a baby! Luckily she's perfect!

Lulu Pahlson–Moller Had another baby, Oliver, born in September 2014. Still living in Battersea.

Clementine Pain Still living in Hampshire with husband and spaniel and definitely not missing the law!

Elizabeth Pollitt Still working at Westonbirt as a PE teacher. Been there five years now! Don't know where the time has gone. Now living in Cirencester and loving it.

Rosalind Price I'm still living in London and still working as a town planning consultant at Gerald Eve.

Laura Sims Still living in Monmouth, South Wales, with hubby and four lovely children.

Frankie Somerset Am still living in Sydney, and we are waiting for the birth of our first baby. Hopefully due any day now.

Becca Williams Am living in Gloucestershire and have started a PR company about a year ago.

Section 70 (2001)
Section representative:
Catharine Loveridge (Hallpike)

Fiona Cameron I am living in Putney and am now a High Jewellery Designer at Garrard (HQ Mayfair). As part of my job, I designed the medals for the Invictus Games, and I am going to be exhibiting a New High jewellery collection in Doha and Basel this year.

Catharine Loveridge (Hallpike) I am still living in Suffolk with James, teaching at a country prep school called Orwell Park and living in Wickham Market. We now have a little girl called Rose, who was born at the end of April last year.

Abby Moule (Warn) We are having a good year; we've moved from London to Chichester and bought our first home. We now have two little girls with our newest daughter being 5 weeks old. Peter and I celebrate our fifth wedding anniversary this year. I am working as a freelance consultant in commercial kitchen design and operations setting up restaurants. I'm having a break from it at the moment with our new baby but will be back to it later this year.

Section 69 (2000)

Section representative:
Lucy Croysdill (Fletcher)

Laura Arnott (Griffiths) My biggest news last year was the birth of my son, Henry, in December. After his arrival, we left Montgomery, Alabama and moved to Hawaii with Stephen's job. It's now my plan to be a stay-at-home mum for a few years, but I hope to do an online Masters and update my skillset. I keep in touch with a few girls from my year and hope to catch up with several of them on my infrequent trips back to the UK.

Lucy Croysdill (Fletcher) We moved to our new house in Tunbridge Wells last August. Nina is now two years old, and I returned to work at the beginning of 2014. I am working four days a week from home for a company called Roxhill Media. I keep in touch with quite a few Westonbirt girls on a regular basis. Even though we might not be on the same continent, Skype and WhatsApp make it very easy!

Lucinda Davy Working for a Swiss family investment office in Mayfair, London since 2012, still living with Henny Mercer. Recently engaged to a naval architect who also works in London, to be married this year.

Clemmie Jacques Where to start… I haven't given news in a while so this is going to be more than a few lines, sorry. But it's an interesting story to tell.

I'll start with my current course. I'm doing my Doctorate in Counselling Psychology, final year. All I have left to complete is my research thesis. In order to get on this course I had to get years of work experience and even did two MScs; as it's an extremely competitive course, and life experience counts for much when working in this field. I have had several placements during this course: Forensic Mental Health services in a secure unit, University College London Hospital, IAPT in Newham, MIND counselling service in Tower Hamlets, and presently at the Gender Identity Clinic, Charing Cross Hospital. So I can specialise in several areas: Gender and Sexual Identity, Addiction Services, Personality Disorders, Community Mental Health, and much more.

I decided to become a counselling psychologist after my own struggle with mental health. It's not been easy, it has taken me a while, but I will get there and be stronger for my experience. I wanted to give something back to society, increase the quality of treatments on offer, reduce the stigma around this subject, and, at some point, try to do my part in improving the NHS options for those suffering from mental health problems.

I also still enjoy doing a bit of acting, stand-up comedy and singing in a choir which I helped found last year. No marriage or babies as yet, but I still have time, and I have lots of godchildren who keep the broodiness at bay! If I say any more, I'll be at risk of boring you, but if anyone wants to talk more about what I've been up to, or even pick my brains about mental health and further education, I'd be happy to hear from you.

Cindy Kar I am living in Hong Kong, I am married and have two boys. One is nearly three, and one is four months old.

Michelle Lawson I'm still living and working in Boston, USA. I see a lot of **Eila**, **Lucy**, **Henny**, **Lucinda**, **Laura** and **Bex**. I travel back and forth to Europe quite a lot visiting friends, family and my boyfriend.

Poppy Morgan I have just changed jobs to become a Director at Savills Commercial to head up a fund for their Property and Asset Management Department. I live in Putney and am into my sailing, I am a skipper and do various trips in the Solent and the Med as well as some racing. I am on the Offshore Yacht committee for London Corinthians Sailing Club and organise the overseas trips. This year our biggest trip is going to Vancouver for two weeks sailing up into the Desolation Sound - five yachts in total are going in September.

Section 68 (1999)
Section representative:
New representative needed
If you'd like to volunteer, please contact Leigh Ralphs via the school
There is consequently no news from Section 68 this year -
let's hope for a bumper update in the next edition!

Section 67 (1998)
Section representative:
Julia Collis (Bleasdale)

Julia Collis (Bleasdale) I have enjoyed the past year, continuing to live in Wiltshire and being kept busy by my two children. My son, Tobias, continues to love being in the Nursery at Westonbirt Prep and is excited by the prospect of Reception there in September. Isabel will be 2 in June and is turning into a lovely little girl. Recently **Rose Haines (Chadwyck-Healey)** got in touch. It was super to meet up and catch up on over 10 years of news. My sister **Olivia** got married at Westonbirt last April. It was a wonderful day, the school looked amazing and family and friends who had not been to Westonbirt before could easily see why we have such happy memories. Recently we attended a ball at school. It was lovely to see **Mrs Henderson** there, and it also brought back amusing memories, as my father dropped us off, which had not happened since the Leavers' Ball!

Kate Eckley Kate wrote to say that she is now living in Shipton Moyne and so is very close to School. Kate is working for Burges Salmon in Bristol.

Section 66 (1997)
Section representative:
Katie Mason (Eves)

Polly Allen (Mann) is managing some work and had a new addition to the family in 2014 with the arrival of Lara, a sister to Sam and Isla. Life is busy but fun.

Louise Banerjee (Barnwell) is still working as Head of Geography at an independent school in Northamptonshire. She enjoys teaching Geography, whilst also coaching sport on a regular basis, though unfortunately no lacrosse! She lives with her husband Robin and her daughter in a local village and loves the rural life. Her daughter, Lyla, is now nearly two and keeping everyone on their toes, including her grandparents (Louise's parents) who live in the same village!

Anna Charlton is still living in Walthamstow and enjoying freelancing - never a dull moment. Looking forward to becoming an aunt in July!

Zarina Chatwin (Marsh) is still living in sunny California. Caspar (4), Ottilia (2) and Atticus (1) seem to be growing up too fast.

Laura Corbett (Cooper) can't quite believe where the time has gone and how her responsibilities have grown! Jack arrived in November 2014, welcomed by his big sister Emilia, now three. Juggling motherhood, whilst managing the family dairy farm at Avebury is fairly crazy, hence her lack of communication via Facebook!

Sally Cullum (Hopwell) has just completed the Association of Accounting Technicians (AAT) qualification and has worked in the accounts department for Boughton Estates Ltd for over four years.

Jess Green (White) Jake and Rosie are growing up fast and have just turned two. She is still working as a GP, which is very busy, so relieved to be working only three days a week. They're spending lots of time down in Wiltshire and hoping to move there soon.

Sally Hoare After 10 years in Sydney, she decided to pack everything up and move to Bangkok to do the marketing for a bicycle tour operator called Spice Roads. She is enjoying the crazy city but misses her early morning swims down at Bondi Beach.

Pea Lawson ((Petronella) Gordon-Dean) has been in Miami for six years and finally has a Green Card to go with the American passport-holding children. They are now two and three, and they are exploding out of their flat and decamping to suburbia later this year. Pea says please get in touch if you are in Florida!

Katie Mason (Eves) is back at work part-time, so again happily getting out to Africa albeit less often than before. Currently managing malaria and neglected tropical disease programmes in Angola and otherwise playing with Cecily, her 14 month old daughter, and hanging out with husband and dog in the Cotswolds.

Marina Souter She is still living in London, and very excited about setting up her own company as a consultant for party planning, event catering and project managing events.

Anna-Claire Temple (Filer) is currently living in Bristol, balancing a demanding but very enjoyable job as deputy CEO of a small charity with being a mum to four-year-old energetic twin boys Jamie and Noah.

Anne Van Schrader has now been living in London for the last five years after spending two wonderful sunny years in Madrid. Anne is working for Visa heading up their payment network strategy and enjoying the challenge, whilst also travelling from time to time across Europe with work. 2015 has already been a good year in terms of seeing and spending time with fun Westonbirt faces from Cornwall, Somerset and London.

Samantha Vermaak (Russell) She and her husband are finally moving into their first owned house! Very exciting, it's a bit of a project, so should keep them entertained. Still TB Vaccine Programme Manager at Oxford University; the job is hectic but interesting and she keeps herself even more busy with a ridiculous number of hobbies as well as fundraising. Last year was a 40 mile walk (tortuous - not doing that again) and the Oxfam Emergency Challenge (tough but fun). She hopes you're all well and enjoying life.

Section 65 (1996)
Section representative:
Catherine Hirons (Charlton)

Charlotte Avery (Pounder) I'm still enjoying living in Newbury with Brian and the boys, Euan (10) and Jacob (6). Work is going well - I'm still a Therapeutic Radiographer, but I'm in more of a management role, mainly responsible for staff training, although I'm still let loose on patients every now and again. I spend my spare time ferrying the boys to their numerous activities or running. I've entered into a few more half marathons this year so that should keep me busy.

Alexandra Butler (Earley) It's been a year since we moved out of Bristol and we're really enjoying village life. Not completely cut off from the city as still working in Bristol part time. I've just limped into my 16th year at Hargreaves Lansdown. Our elder daughter started school last year, and the little one is starting pre-school in Westonbirt later this year – in what was formerly the San!

Felicity Cadwallader Same flat share (still in Highbury), same search to buy somewhere in London (still seemingly impossible), same job (still with Thomas Cook), same man (still in Birmingham!) Happy and well, which is the important thing.

Rachel Carey (Kidd) Big move for us this year, as we are putting everything into storage in Australia, and myself, my hubby and the dog (aka my baby!) are returning to the UK and Europe for an indefinite period of time! All very exciting. I have missed my family and 'home' for the past 13 years and now the time is right for us to return. I have landed myself a job at Ewen Manor for June and July, so I am now desperately looking for furnished accommodation in the area! The lovely **Claire O'Gorman** has been trying to help me out but if anyone else has any ideas please let me know. Looking forward to reconnecting when I am home. My Facebook is 'Rachael Sarah Kidd' for those of you who don't have it already as it will be the best form of contact!

Nicola Chapman (Oliver-Bellasis) We have had an exciting year. We bought our 'forever home' nr Newbury, which needs a lot of work. Tom is going to project manage, although I will help with the important decisions over the kitchen and bathrooms. I had a baby, Amelia, who was born at the beginning of February so my hands are rather full. She is scrummy and I'm loving being a mummy. I am enjoying maternity leave having been teaching in a village school.

Fiona Christie (Thorne) Since last year, Rosie and Emily's new sister 'baby Bea' arrived so we now have three little girls. Life is full on with three children under the age of four, but lovely! Still a full-time mum living in London which we love, but starting to think about moving out to the sticks soon. Just got to work out where to go! See lots of **Issy**, **Lucy** and **Claire**.

Laura Cristau Having had a very busy year last year, I have been terrible at keeping in touch with friends, sorry! Started an exciting project in June, in charge of setting up an auction house in Paris. It has been up and running since the end of October, and we've just had a fantastic four-day marathon of auctions selling off an *haute couture* collection at the end of January. With a small group of female friends. we are working on a project for a Christmas market - a lot of DIY involved which should be fun. Besides work and projects and leaking roofs, the rest of my time is dedicated to trying to keep up with my daughter's boundless energy. She's turning five in April and is already planning her guest list for her birthday party, so I think I'm going to have my hands full!

Louisa Gallimore Our little boy Sam is now two and is a handful (in a good way!) He goes to French day care so is already overtaking me in the French linguistics department! We're making the most of the winter and have been up to the snow (Sam hated the snow, liked the hot chocolate and tartiflette) and have just got back from seeing his Aussie family down under.

Laetitia Glossop Incredibly busy 2014 - business going really well, we had a fantastic year and hopefully that will continue in 2015. In the summer I was selected as Conservative Parliamentary Candidate for North Durham. It's the longest held Labour seat in the country with a mere 12,076 majority! A tough challenge, but I'm giving it my best shot and learning new skills like fundraising (seriously hard in a safe Labour seat!), media work and lots of campaigning. Enjoying it enormously, although the next few months through till May are going to be manic!

Claire Hall (Lewis) Still enjoying life in Crowthorne, Berkshire, where I am living with my husband and three kids. The kids are growing fast,

Ryan is 11, Katie 10 and Harry 7. Ryan started secondary school in September (definitely feeling old - it doesn't seem like that long since we were all starting in Sedgwick!)

To add to the chaos, I started work last summer, I work school hours in the village which is fab, but with walking the dog twice a day I haven't got the time to do anything at the moment, so I will wait and see what happens when my contract ends in the summer.

We took the kids skiing in February half term, which was great fun, but we have been home for two weeks now, and are still exhausted! Definitely hoping for a couple of quieter weekends now!

Julia Herbert The last year was mainly spent learning how to keep a small human being alive, existing on zero sleep and pretending that I could continue life as before! I've loved it though. And the reward of a little smiling face makes it all ok. I'm due to go back to work in March, but having failed to negotiate flexi-time with my employers, I'm setting up as a freelance marketing consultant. A little scary on one hand, but mainly exciting. I will be working from home a lot of the time, so to save me talking to the postman, do come to Southfields for lunch!

Lucy Heyworth (Pearson) Can't believe it's been a year since we last all wrote! I have had my second boy, Sam, who is a very happy addition to our family!

Catherine Hirons (Charlton) Having spent six months of last year husbandless while Durham was at sea, it has been blissful having him home - at weekends, at least, as he is now in Swindon for the year. Work is going well - busy as always, (which hospital isn't?), but still really enjoying finally being a consultant and have taken on some new responsibilities which have been challenging in a good way.

We are expecting our first baby in July, which is very exciting - lots to do before then, including finding a forever house which we still haven't managed! We are now looking with renewed vigour and are keeping our fingers crossed the right thing will come on the market very soon! In the meantime we are moving into a Navy property nearby which will be much better. Can see the sea from our sitting room, so can't complain.

Caroline Kearsley (White) I have just spent the weekend with **Emma O'Regan** catching up which was ace. Jo and I have bought a boat and are taking a year off work with the girls to sail around the Med. Jo's sister and brother-in-law live in Montenegro, which is going to be our final destination. We are leaving in June, which I am sure will come around very quickly. Very excited, although a little scared, as I have to do a bit of homeschooling. I am not sure that they are going to learn anything or listen to me at all!

Isabel Langly-Smith (Lowndes) Another year flies by, my baby food business is starting to take off, which is exciting and keeps me very busy. Toby, Sam and Isla are growing up too fast, and I now find myself in the world of school, parents' evenings etc, which I still falsely think I'm too young for!

Diana Lewis I've been in Reigate, Surrey for 18 months now, which has gone by so fast! I'm enjoying living in the south and being able to visit family and friends without it involving a massive drive! I invested in an inflatable kayak last year, and had lots of fun exploring the waterways nearby. We are looking forward to the warmer weather and getting a bit more use out of them again this year (your dog barking at you and chasing you along the riverbank is quite amusing)!

Nicola Marson (Maguire) Edward Raymond Marson was born last October, and we are completely smitten with him. He adores his older brother Guy, who is now three and a half years old, and smiles and giggles at him all the time, however it's taking Guy a little while to get used to Edward. It's a slow road but we're getting there. I'm currently on maternity leave from my graphic design job in London, which I hope to return to later this year.

Alys Mathew Had a pretty amazing year in 2014. Having negotiated my way out of Betfair at the end of 2013, I decided to take some time out and go and do something I'd always wanted to do - a warm weather triathlon camp in Lanzarote. Okay, so not everyone's idea of relaxation and fun, I know, but off I went. LOVED it, the coach was amazing - in fact loved it so much I went back out in April! Over the next 12 weeks I did some token marketing consultancy and loads of training, plus a few competitions (where I saw **Jo Wilkie**! Fab to see her - just like the old days!)

All the hard work paid off when I qualified at a race in May to represent GB at my age group at the World Triathlon Championships in Edmonton, Canada in September. Pretty nutty, and even now I cannot quite get my head round it! Came 17th in the world and was the third British athlete home. This year it starts all over again with Geneva for the Europeans in July and Chicago for the Worlds in September - guess it's one way to see the world!

Sophie Meredith Have had a busy year. Apart from working hard, Tosh and I got engaged in May and married in December which was a crazy time of year for a wedding. I saw **Susie Hall** and **Charlie Rylance** who are both on amazing form. We then headed to the Atlas Mountains for our honeymoon, which was beautiful and exactly the peace and quiet we needed.

Kathryn Morrison (Horner) I am currently studying Nursing on an Access Course, and then I am returning to Portsmouth University in September, 15 years after graduating. This time I will be doing a BSc in Therapeutic Radiography so that I can then work with cancer patients. It is going to be a hard three years, but I'm looking forward to it! Jamie is now 11 and at secondary school which makes me feel ancient and Imogen is 7. My divorce (and freedom!) should be finalised very soon. The 3 of us still live just outside Portsmouth, but I do plan to escape one day after I (hopefully) graduate!

Emma O'Regan (Leadbetter) We are living very happily in Oxfordshire, having found our dream home a couple of years ago and extended it before Christmas. Holly is in her first year at school, although she enjoys it she would always rather be at home, and we miss her when she's there! Zachary is full of boundless energy, and so much fun. I'm working part time as an advisory teacher for the SEN service, having resigned from my deputy head job when I had Zach. Much better work-life balance, but still miss my old school.

We spend most of our holidays travelling in Europe in our camper van (so lucky we all get them together!) Off to tour Scandinavia in the summer, and Portugal at Easter. Still in touch with Holly and Zach's wonderful godmums, **Caroline** and **Emma**, and was so lovely to see **Cherry** earlier this year too.

Claire Poole (O'Gorman) Still got the legal headhunting business and have had one of our busiest years due to the property market being so buoyant. Living in Clapham and Johnny Vaughn is my new neighbour - still slightly in awe of him due to the Big Breakfast infatuation days at school! Jessica started school in September and Alex nursery - don't want them to grow up. Want to freeze this age! Keep in touch with about five of the Westonbirt girls but had a lovely visit/reunion from **Cherry** which was wonderful - hadn't seen her since we were 21, I think!

Hannah Pope (West) I had a baby boy in July, and my eldest started school in September. (Nobody warned me how traumatic the first week would be... for me that is!) I went back to work in January which I love, but life is hectic!

Katie Powell I have given up work to move to the Fens with my boyfriend. I still have my three dogs and now have a pet pig called Beryl!

Nathalie Simpson So after the craziest 18 months ever, I will finally be heading home in May! In that time, I've moved countries twice (New York and Hong Kong), bought a new flat, moved into it, moved out, moved in and moved out again, changed roles three times within the same company, travelled to the most amazing places in South East Asia, had a small accident with a small Harry Potter scar as testament, and met some incredible people! Very much looking forward to catching up with friends and family though and planning my yearly trip to France to see **Natacha** and **Laura**.

Una Strauss (Laffan) Still Living in London. Gave birth to a gorgeous little girl called Grace. We have come to spend some time in Mexico with family - it has been delicious to be in the sunshine instead of deep winter in London, but heading back in April. Enjoying life being a mama.

Cherry Teswosdi I have just opened my own resort, Palm Beach on Pranburi Beach, Prachubkirikan. If anyone would like to visit me here, please let me know.

Frances Von Bonde (Glyn-Owen) I became a mummy to a beautiful little girl five weeks ago. Busy doing our house renovations. even though I've had to take a back seat whilst Ella is so young. I'm sure it won't be too long until she's at one of our projects though!

Venetia Whale (Heesom) We welcomed our son Theodore (Theo) into the world on 2nd February and are in heaven! Juggling running a pub, keeping two dogs and having a baby is a challenge, but one that, so far, is under control!

Jo Wilkie Having worked for the same company for over six years, I've now moved to VitalityLife, still in Financial Services and working with technology, but just on the other side of the fence, as it were. I've gone from an American-owned organisation to a South African one, so my continent of travel has changed, and I am just back from my first trip out to the offices in Jo'Burg. Only a brief trip of three days, with a packed itinerary of work meetings, but I did get to go on a rhino and lion safari. Actually the lions were well hidden, other than the baby ones in the crèche, but we saw loads of other native animals, birds and beautiful butterflies. Vitality sponsor a lot of sporting events, and much of the company ethos is around health, fitness and wellbeing (no coincidence that I ended up working for this company!) so they are sponsoring me in some sporting endeavours and enabling easier access into a number of events.

Which brings me onto the sport… Having had a few persistent knee problems since the Paris Marathon in 2012, I turned to triathlon in 2013 and just a year later qualified to represent Great Britain at the World Age Group Championship in Canada (2014). Unfortunately I had to turn down my place, but **Alys** can tell you all about it, as she has been doing the same thing and did compete in Canada.

Funny that our paths should cross again, and we bumped into each other at the British Triathlon Championships in Liverpool (taking place whilst Hurricane Bertha hit – not fun!) and have both qualified to go to Geneva for the European Championships in July of this year, and this time I am definitely taking up my place! No doubt we'll see each other at an event before then!

Just a couple of weeks ago I was at Westonbirt giving a careers talk to the Sixth Form and catching up with a few other former pupils and teachers that are still there, after all these years! Mrs Dunn had done a fantastic job organising the whole event and was in absolutely fine form, and Mrs Phillips came along to support and was proudly telling me about her grandchildren (four I think it is now) and reprimanding me for not doing any art! I didn't know any of the younger ones that were presenting but did remember **Claire Galer (Dorman)** and **Cordelia Gover (Harries)** from the years above.

All is well at home in Withington (rural Gloucestershire/ Cotswolds), living with boyfriend Dave and Hobbes our dog. We've now lived here just over a year and have spent the last 12 months doing a few things to the house, which has entailed some spending, which in turn has curtailed snowboarding holidays for this season, so not much to report on that front.

Section 64 (1995)

Section representative:
Emma Lloyd-Williams
There is no news from Section 64 this year -
let's hope for a bumper update in the next edition!

Section 63 (1994)

Section representative:
Jemima Mann

Ruth Baker Guy and I have moved back to the UK after four fabulous years in Australia and are now settled in Hertfordshire. Life is dominated by three children and a crazy dog. Planning a reunion for all of our year group in a London pub in August. I will communicate via email and Facebook. Looking forward to seeing as many of you as possible.

Bryonie Clarendon (Leask) Living in Hampshire with George and my three boys.

Victoria Edwards (Holland) I finally made the move out of London to Oxfordshire and am loving the country air, (but less so the daily commute to London). Eldest daughter now started school (am feeling old) and a big birthday end of this year (feeling even older). I still keep in touch with quite a few – one of my daughter Annabel's school friends' mums turned out to be **Cordelia Harris** from two years above us. What a small world!

Claire Ferrige My news is that I still live in Alaro, Mallorca - been here for nearly 13 years now. I am the manager of a super yacht management company and have two boys aged six and three. My husband also works in yachting and is an engineer, so he travels away a fair bit (he is mid-Atlantic as I write this). My boys go to an international Spanish school, and my eldest already speaks excellent Spanish. By the time school is done, they will be trilingual, which is fantastic, I have also had to learn Spanish, but it is not so easy later in life!

Lucy Fey (Clark) I am still living in Bristol. My children are now eight, and I can't believe how quickly time has flown! In September, I started teaching at my daughters' school, part time. I am really enjoying having more time to be a mum. Since I took a step back, I am now wondering how on earth I managed to work full-time and get everything done! I'm loving every minute of it.

Alyx Gerrards (Swain) Still living near Manchester and running my own HR Consultancy. Married for 14 years with two children, Sam (9) and Amelia (6). Life is very busy but good.

Nancy Lawson (White) The B&B is going well, and I now let out six bedrooms, and host small meetings for The National Trust and Nationwide. We have also just submitted planning to convert a barn into a large meeting room and party barn to hire out. Hopefully we will be able to do it. George and Zara are in great form and keeping me on my toes. Perce is still working for Knight Frank. I have decided this year to walk an ultra-Marathon – 60 miles in one go for charity. I need a challenge and an excuse to escape work – although slightly worried this may be too far! Hope you are all well. Please call in if you are passing.

Jemima Mann Still pretending I am still in my twenties and spending time doing different jobs in different countries to deal with my low boredom threshold. I am currently in New Zealand, but also work in England, France and Gibraltar at different times of the year.

Belle Morton I am living in Hong Kong but find myself increasingly working in mainland China. Recently saw **Sharifa**, **Bada**, **Tory** and **Ruth** and determined to catch up with **Clare Cameron (Ferrige)** this year!

Sharifa Parker (Taylor) Living in West Byfleet working out how to fit in work and looking after two kids without going crazy!

Sam Sant I'm living in the Cotswolds, married and have two kids, one of each (the boy is not yet 1). I spent my 20s and early 30s basically moving around a lot. I am currently working as a Marketing Manager but doing a Psychology degree with a view to doing something in that field.

Section 62 (1993)
Section representative:
Joanna Runcimann

Alice Clarke (Kealey) Andrew has retired from the Army after 16 years, so we've left Oman and are now living in Bermuda with his new job! Think we'll be here for three years. No more babies - stuck firm at Violet, Margot and Fergus, now 7, 6 and 4. I have lots of time on my hands now that all my babies go to school. I'm well into a primal/paleo/ancestral health way of life and am doing a course with the Institute for Transformational Nutrition in the vain hope that I might soon discover what I want to do when I grow up! Every now and then I hand-sew a quilt, dig out a linocut or chop down overgrown plants in my sea-view garden. Other than that I watch rubbish TV and try hard not to drink too much coffee.

Caroline Copland Life continues apace. I have now tipped over the 40 hill, but did so in style at the top of the Wellington Arch 40 years to the day that I was born within 100m of the spot. I was thrilled to share the moment with fabulous family and friends, including **Chloe** and **Cara**.

Work continues to keep me overly busy, having joined with JLL in October 2014 and now have a number of very exciting challenges ahead as marketing director within a global real estate firm currently focusing on the residential UK market. It's an unforeseen and yet enjoyable opportunity to learn more about my father's career, much of what I touch today being linked to projects he was involved in during the 60s, 70s and 80s, including the regeneration of Carnaby Street where I lunch every day!

Losing my darling mother to a brain tumour last September has been hard, but we had wonderful shared experiences during her short illness and were lucky to be able to. Socially and romantically - as full on and challenging as ever, but isn't 40 a great time to learn about life?!

Chloe Horner (Hignett) Angus, Ivo and I are now living in Blewbury in Oxfordshire to be near Harwell Campus where Angus' work is now based. We are really enjoying life here. I am a full-time mother and still working as a designer. I hope you are well, and a collective happy 40th birthday to you all!

Joanna Runciman (Oliver-Bellasis) We are still living in British Columbia, Canada. I am writing my second book, this time on decluttering and simplifying life. My husband Andrew is currently injured (whilst ski instructing), broken leg and knee, but with surgery will no doubt be back on skis next winter. A happy outdoors lifestyle. I enjoy lots of walking, biking and being part of a small community. I am also making my own skincare which I give to friends at this point, but who knows if it will grow into something else in the future. Life is good; I am happier being 40 than I ever was when younger! So I suppose life does begin at 40.

Caroline van Kuffeler (Morris) We finally left London after years of talking about it and have moved to Wiltshire. We're only six weeks in, but absolutely loving country life, and I feel so much more relaxed! The girls, Willa (3½) and Anoushka (2) are having some amazing early biology lessons, as we've rented a house on a working farm where lambs are being born on a daily basis. **Sam Shaw**'s father is my next-door neighbour, so Sam has been over with her daughter Elsa who is exactly the same age as Willa. Making lovely new friends who have been incredibly welcoming and have various very old friends nearby. Hugo is commuting to London every day, which is tough, but he insists worth it. I am standing down as our Section Rep and handing over to **Jo Runciman** who has very kindly offered to take over so she will be in touch next year. Oh, and a very happy 40th to everyone this year!

Alison Williams Not really any new news here. Still living in Congresbury (between Bristol and Weston-super-Mare) with Craig and Rhiannon (8) and Callum (5). Still working for Langford Vet Services in their diagnostic labs. On my 40th birthday I was sad enough to go for a tour round Westonbirt with Craig. Only Miss Gould there now from our times. Shame the silk wall coverings were falling off in many places, but other than that, I thought it all looked pretty much the same. Hope to see you all again one day. **Hillary Jam**es over from Oz and offering to meet any one for a picnic at Forest of Dean or Westonbirt 27th June. I said I'd go.

Section 61 (1992)
Section representative:
Caroline Walker

Leila Bliss (Wigan) Nothing new or interesting to add - just mum to three very demanding small people! Considering going back to work soon though for some life of my own and sanity! Hope you are all well.

Cordelia Gover (Harries) I've enjoyed catching up with lots of Section 61 friends over the year as there have been quite a few 40th birthday celebrations, including my own in the summer. It was great to see so many of you: **Caroline Walker**, **Claire Dorman**, **Caroline Pullin**, **Melanie Hobson**, **Deborah Pain**, **Rachael Pain**, **Candy Barnett**, **Deborah Dereham**, and **Antonia Cridland**. I've also seen **Charlie Hunt**, **Note**, **Sam Neary**, **Claire Guy** and quite a lot of **Katie Crofts**.
    Both my girls, Jazzy (6) and Eleanor (4) are now at school, so I'm enjoying a bit more time to myself and have got a pony to keep me on my toes! He joins the rest of my furry family (a dog, two cats, two bunnies, three fish and 16 wild ducks!
    I was very honoured recently and was invited to speak at the Inspiring Women Day to the Sixth Form students. It was a lovely day and especially nice seeing a few teachers that I recognised like Mrs Phillips and Mrs Dunn on the day.

Charlotte Haynes (Hunt) Happy 40th to everyone over the last year – we made it! Hope everyone enjoyed their celebrations. I had a fabulous party and was lucky to be joined by WB friends to celebrate. **Harriet Taylor (Ferguson)** may be moving back to the Bath area, so hoping to catch up if this happens. Always happy to catch up with friends if they're in the area – give me a shout and call in! Ben, Felix and I are happy and enjoying an ever-busy life. I feel very lucky and privileged to have such fab friends from school and that we're all still in touch. Love to everyone and love hearing everyone's news.

Virginia Kelly We now have two children, a boy of 3 (nearly 4) and a one-year-old girl. We moved last summer to Malvern Wells to a converted chapel on the side of the Malvern Hills. It's lovely here, and we're all well and happy. Doing a bit of freelance business affairs work for a couple of small independent TV drama producers and otherwise spending lots of time with my family. Have seen **Coquita** recently and also keep in touch with **Henrietta**, **Leila** and **Poppy**.

Lara Masters Spent the past year fighting for planning permission, going to appeal, winning and finally starting to build the house in our garden that I will be living in, with my husband, in the summer. Very time-consuming and stressful, much harder than *Grand Designs*! But it will be worth it, and then everyone is invited over for housewarming, one at a time though, as there won't be enough room to swing a cat, but it will be gorgeous and ours!

As for Westonbirt girls, I am still very much in touch and very much in love with **Vers (Verity)** and **Pops**. Also, finally caught up with fabulous **Harry Taylor (Ferguson)** after a gap of over 20 years. It was fascinating and most enlightening comparing our different experiences of WB shenanigans and we will definitely keep in touch.

Rachael Terry (Pain) Still living in Odiham, Hampshire, and I have set up my own small niche recruitment consultancy business last year which seems to be going well. I'm also juggling that with two busy boys, Edward (8) and Henry (6) at school and all their extra-curricular activities. Lots of sport for the boys to keep them busy! All good fun! I have put my tennis coaching on the back burner (I realised I wasn't going to quite make it like Judy Murray!) but still love playing when I get a chance.

Alice Townsend I continue to live at Newbottle, South Northamptonshire, and run the family farm. I have had a really up-and-down year in 2014. I lost my lovely old dog Bracken in the summer, which was very sad, but she was pretty old and ill and had a great life so that was a consolation. We then got the great news that my mother, **Juliet Townsend** (who was also an old Westonbirt girl) had been made a Dame in the Queen's Honours. She was thrilled, and it was, in my opinion, thoroughly deserved after many years working as Lady-in-Waiting to Princess Margaret, and then serving as Lord Lieutenant of Northamptonshire for over 15 years. So in October, accompanied by my sisters and father, she made her way down to Windsor Castle to pick up her medal, which was all really exciting. I was not able to accompany them as I was in hospital giving birth to my son Toby on the same day!

Unfortunately, Mum had been struggling with various health problems for a couple of years and was diagnosed with cancer in the spring. After all the excitement of Windsor and Toby, she really took a dive, and only four weeks after Toby was born, she passed away. I am so sad that she is not here to see Toby grow up but I am also so glad she knew he had arrived safely. So bittersweet really.

So far, being a Mum has been fantastic, and I am really pleased as Toby seems to be doing well now - he is so grown up at four months old! Hope all is well with everyone else.

Caroline Walker I've completed my four year Masters in Integrative Child and Adolescent Psychotherapy and Counselling, although I am currently finishing off my dissertation and *viva*. So, I'm hoping to be a qualified and accredited Child and Adolescent Psychotherapist soon – it's been a long journey but a rewarding one. After returning from Dublin, my partner has acquired a job near Windsor, so I spend half my time there and half at my place in the country. When I have managed to get my head out of my books, I have seen **Caroline Pullin**, **Melanie Hobson**, **Charlie Hunt**, **Corks Harries**, **Candy Barnet**, **Sam Neary**, **Deborah Dereham**, **Claire Dorman**, **Debs Pain**, **Rachael Pain** and **Clare Guy** this year. It's great to keep in touch with everyone.

Caroline Wilson (Pullin) All well and happy, but very busy as always. Two boys giving Geoff and I much pleasure, they are now 4 and 7. Still working as a chartered surveyor in my own business, which I run from the farm part-time with juggling family and farm. Thanks to Cordelia's party last summer I saw lots of old WBs, which really was lovely - thank you Corks! I keep in touch with **Melanie** and **Lina** quite regularly and love seeing **Charlie**'s and others' updates on Facebook!

Section 60 (1991)
Section representative:
Rebecca Willows
There is no news from Section 54 this year -
let's hope for a bumper update in the next edition!

Section 59 (1990)
Section representative:
Julia Roberts (Stubblefield)

Harriet Bruce (Grove) Last summer we bought the house in Edinburgh we had been renting for a couple of years, and are about to start a fairly major programme of improvements. We will have to move out for some of the time, which will be interesting logistically, as I run my bookkeeping business from home! Hopefully it will all be worthwhile, and we will be finished in time to host Christmas. Our two boys, Oliver (10) and Alex (9) are both enjoying their music, much to my delight. They play violin and piano, so I have great hopes for Bruce family piano trios in the years to come.

Emily Reed (Hogarth) I decided to take a bit of a big leap into the unknown last summer and left the company I had run for two and a half years and set up Dance Grooves. Dance Grooves specialise in street dance classes and parties, mainly for children but our parties aren't limited to street dance, currently working on a concept for cheerleading parties! We launched Alphabet Dance in January for toddlers and pre-schoolers, and we have just been booked by Gambado Chelsea to run events and classes at their fantastic venue by Chelsea Harbour. Loving running my own business, it's so rewarding but lots of hard work too.

Cosima turns 9 in May and Enzo turns 6 in July, they are just growing up too fast but we are loving every moment, precious and super fun times. Currently on countdown to our annual family ski holiday over Easter.

Julia Roberts (Stubblefield) I set up on my own last year as a virtual PA, working from home. It's going really well, loads of different, varied clients in weird and wonderful industries which makes work much more interesting. It enables me to work around the kids' school activities and pick-ups, but hoping to work on the quality me-time part next! We finished the house build last December, so enjoying the rewards of open plan space (apart from the noise!) Just need to sort out the garden and rest of the house now.

The kids are doing well. My eldest, Lucas, has just got into a local grammar school after much angst of the 11+. Working out if Mattie is up to it too. Libby joins Mattie at his school in September, which is very exciting. Hoping to set up another London reunion at some point before or after the summer holidays.

Section 58 (1989)
Section representative:
Natasha McLeod (Marsh)

Natasha McLeod Marsh A small group of us – **Eleanor Findlater (Davies), Kate Anstis (Auckland), Sophie Hughues Despointes (Baile de Laperrière)** and **Audrey Boss** along with our families went to the Old Girls' Carol Service in the London last December and it was absolutely brilliant. The school went to so much effort to make it a lovely event and the soppy ones amongst us (me) had to fight back the tears when the Chamber Choir sang. We had lunch beforehand so we could all catch up and then dashed across the square to the church. I can't recommend it highly enough for those of you who didn't make it.

Chantal Michelin (Lane) has produced a stunning photo book of our years at Westonbirt (1982-1989), and the back cover has listed buzz words that all Westonbirt girls from our era would recognise, for example - "tuck shop, Hades, Mr and Mrs Christmas Pudding, Upper 4 Nannies, Vespers, Wing Commander Watts, For What We Are About To Receive, Dom Work, End of Term Riots, Get Off The Grass etc." The book is priceless and a wonderful reminder of our happy years at Westonbirt.

Ione started school last September and she is very happy, which is a relief. I volunteer with the Year 1s for one morning a week, and I love it. It's a great way to understand how the school works, get to know the children and see what Ione has in store for her next year. I am still running the toddler group on another morning. Flora has another year to go before starting school but I need to start thinking about what I am going to do with all that spare time (!) once she starts.

Section 57 (1988)
Section representative:
Fiona Stokes (Tobin)

Sarah Green (Gladdish) Still a consultant physician on the Isle of Wight. NHS is not a great place to be at the moment. Foolishly started doing MSc but it finishes in July, so on final push now. Husband Adrian long suffering as I grumble my way through MSc. Max 16, doing GCSEs – fingers crossed; Bella 14, just started at Canford; Tobin 7, enjoying Beavers.

Holly Hunter (Bentall) Nothing changes too much in our busy household. Another working cocker, Lola, arrived before Christmas, and a pony for our daughter Selina looks imminent. We spent 10 days prior to Christmas in Mauritius celebrating my parents' fiftieth wedding anniversary and my mother's seventieth birthday, which was fun. Took Selina to Bekonscot Model Village last summer with **Wendy Duckworth's (Greey)** two boys Arthur and Bertie. Hoping to drop into Westonbirt when we are visiting for Badminton in May.

Michele Paolini (Crane) I still live in Udine, Italy with my husband and two boys. Nicolas is 14 and Max is 13. Both of them are already way taller than me now. I don't have much family left in the UK so I don't come over very often unfortunately, although every so often I do a flying visit to Bristol to see my goddaughter and friends.

Amanda Spring My last 12 months have been rather hectic, I am now living between Budapest and Warsaw, both of which I love but not quite sure where is home yet. I still keep in touch with **Katherine Jory (Hunt)** who has two lovely little girls. Sadly my Father died yesterday morning, [26 February] but I was with him, and it was painless, so I was thankful for that. I hope everyone else is well and happy.

Sally Togneri (Upton) We are all well. I'm enjoying working part time and playing as much tennis as I can; Dave is running the Brighton marathon this year. Alice (8) and Beth (7) are delightful and have started a new school together at Gateway in Great Missenden which we are really pleased with. We are enjoying getting away in our motorhome, as well as friends and family and home of course. My sister **Lindsay Upton** is really well and enjoying some fabulous holidays with her husband. We see quite a lot of them. All good really - long may it continue!

Jenny Watson (Stubbs) I'm still living in Cork, working for myself as a medical secretary. Sadly we lost both my father and father-in-law within nine days of each other last August, whilst we were on holiday in the States, so we've had a tough time. My mother is still in the nursing home in Cheshire, where she was with my father, and she loves it there. I try and get over every few months to see her, but have obviously seen her more frequently of late.

Am in touch with WB old girls on Facebook, and will catch up with **Rachel Cairns** again this summer in Mallorca.

My daughter has her confirmation in a couple of weeks' time (mid-March), and then she prepares to start secondary school in September (they start two years later than the UK in Ireland). Sadly my recent diagnosis of rheumatoid arthritis and lupus has put a stop to many of my hobbies and housework, but I have recently started another new treatment which hopefully will work, and then I'll be back on track! I now sing with two choirs, which keeps me very busy indeed, and one of the choirs has been chosen as the choir to sing at the forthcoming José Carreras and Katherine Jenkins concert in Cork in June!

Section 56 (1987)
Section representative:
Fiona Stokes (Tobin)

Arabella Bishop I am still working away for Sotheby's and living in Dublin – not much has changed then! Hoping to make it over for the lacrosse match for **Celia Graham.**

Georgina Busch (Bryon) Been a busy year, my eldest started secondary school in September. Been quite an adjustment for him as having to be more responsible for himself, but hopefully he'll get the hang of it in due course. In November my husband started a new job for Swedbank based in Stockholm, so if all goes well we'll be joining him there at the end of the school year, including the cat and dog! An exciting prospect as we're looking forward to enjoying the outdoor lifestyle and living near the sea. Still in touch with **Alexandra Trowbridge (Ferguson)** and **Amanda Dekker (Barker-Davies)**.

Victoria Calder All things the same for me, apart from now teaching at a small independent school ranging from reception to sixth form.

Hetty Clark (Bowden) Married to Rich for 21 (scary!) years. Four children: Charlie (15), Angus (14), Poppy (10), Orlando (9). Living in Hillesley. Still visiting Westonbirt once or twice a week for swimming and the sports centre. Run a pentathlon club based at the school - often sit on the wall of the car park (now not allowed!) watching children run. Still remember standing on it while listening to Live Aid. Life involves ferrying children, looking after their horses, standing on the side of assorted pitches - and loving it! In touch with **Mary Scott** regularly but also various people through Facebook. Also going, occasionally, to Book Club run by **Mrs Thombs,** the English teacher who inspired a lifelong love of books.

Helen Curtis (Senior Stern) Helen is very busy running The Jolly Huntsman pub in Kington St Michael, Wiltshire. *[Your section rep is hoping to stay there in June 2015 following a family wedding in Crudwell, near Malmesbury. She might look up **Juliana Nash (Blanch)** at the same time, as Jules lives in Crudwell.]*

Juliet Davidson Not many changes. Still working in the world of cricket. After 10 years with the International Cricket Council, I've now been with the England and Wales Cricket Board for the last 4 years. I'm keeping a low profile at the moment due to our rather poor form in the ICC Cricket World Cup currently taking place in Australia and New Zealand. Hopefully our team's performance will improve and we'll make the quarter finals.

I moved back to London five years ago and have rediscovered my love for this great city, except for the hour commute across the city each morning and evening. I've been playing lots of tennis at my local club and have a busy social life catching up with friends who either still live in London, have returned to London, or are just passing through! I try to get away on one big holiday each year. Last year was Ethiopia which was beautiful and fascinating. I'm still sorting through my 3,000 photos, so next trip not yet planned. A love of mountains and trekking has taken me to all sorts of locations and on many adventures.

Elizabeth Warner (Glen) *[Libby's younger daughter died aged 15 in February 2012, after an accident at home. The following is her first (and very brave) news submission since her bereavement].* I left work in May last year to spend time with the family and grieve for my daughter without any workplace distractions. I love teaching but it can be demanding and stressful, with tests, exams, marking and reports. I prefer a calmer life at the moment. I am now the mother of a 21-year-old daughter. She is at university studying Psychology and French. She went to France for a few weeks last year and loved it. My youngest daughter would have turned 18 last year. Shortly before her birthday, her urn, which we had commissioned, was delivered. We spent her birthday at the beach which was one of her favourite places. After leaving work, I began my Masters degree in Theology, and I hope to go into university lecturing eventually. I have learnt Hebrew, well, some Hebrew! My area of interest is first century Judaism, so Hebrew is a must.

We visited the UK for a month over Christmas, first time back since 2008. I was quite surprised by the changes in the high street and had forgotten how cold it could be. We got back here and a 40-degree heatwave began within a couple of weeks which certainly hit us hard.

I am now President of the South Australian chapter of The Compassionate Friends, a support group for bereaved parents. I also continue to fundraise for the hospital which cared for my daughter in her final week, in memory of her, as well as to say thank you. Money raised goes to the Intensive Care Unit and Neurological Medical Research.

I keep in touch with **Rebecca Jasper**, as she used to be, which is lovely. We're planning to move next year and will probably build our new home. We're just trying to agree on location.

Section 55 (1986)
Section representative:
Fiona Stokes (Tobin)

Joanna Copland 2014 was a difficult year. My darling mother was diagnosed with a brain tumour in January and very sadly died on 5th September. Losing her has left a huge hole in our lives but we take comfort that she was relatively well for about seven months, so as a family we were able to do many special things together and make the most of the time we had. She had supported my father's involvement with Westonbirt for many years and it was lovely to see both **Gillian Hylson-Smith** and **Mary Henderson** at her Thanksgiving Service.

On a more positive note I acquired a black labrador in July. During my mother's final weeks she loved watching the puppy play and Tinta has brought many smiles to the dark days. She comes into school with me each day, and it seems there is always a child at my office door asking to play with her. Long term I hope she will join the Bark and Read programme, helping children who struggle with literacy, but she needs to get over adolescent delinquency first! Otherwise life is busy and a good balance of work and play. I am still in touch with a couple of old girls and hope to visit the school again before too long.

Helen Dugdale I have now been in Leominster for just over a year having moved into my bungalow, with the river at the bottom of the garden, in January 2014. I am able to walk to work, which is great, and have the choice of both a long or shorter route. I work at English Salvage which is a reclamation yard where you are likely to find anything from a vintage light switch to an entire gothic window. We ship UK and worldwide and have a diverse range of clients. Five minutes is never long enough to search our yard or even browse our website!

Outside work, I still enjoy watching sport and now that I am settled, I am going to try and get back to playing some. There is a local rounders team which I may try, and I will probably find myself doing some cricket scoring over the summer months!

Life is good and busy - still haven't managed to get to any more Westonbirt events but you never know what 2015 may hold!

Theresa Hawkins (Cripps) Still living in London near Putney/Barnes and loving it. My two boys, Jack (13) and Freddie (11), have moved on to secondary school and both go to Hampton School. My daughter Lucy (8) is still at St Mary's Primary School in Putney and I co-ordinate the running of the PTA. I finish this summer after two years. I walked 50 kilometres for Alzheimer's on the Thames Path Challenge last year which was great. I seem to do lots of charity things! We have had wonderful holidays this past year, with lots of special birthday celebrations. My husband Richard turned 50, and we used it as an excuse to celebrate a lot! We have seen loads of family and friends, and are all happy and healthy. I stay in touch with the lovely Westonbirt girls mainly via Facebook.

Emma Lack (Fitch) Life has been rather interesting in the Lack Household over the last two years or so, as William (my husband) has been battling two life-threatening conditions. As a result I am back at work in the family business, but still able to be around for the children as much as possible.

Harry (10) headed off to a weekly boarding school in September and is loving it. He is learning to beat his dyslexia and dyspraxia, as well as shooting (terrifying thought) and banging the drums. Fenella (7) has now started playing the flute and we have great fun practising together (I'm almost as rusty as my flute these days) and Olly (5 in April) is loving Reception and having his big sister at school to keep an eye on him. William is amazing - cancer beaten into remission (of course he had to go and get a really rare one!), and we now work on the other issues caused by an unprovoked DVT and pulmonary embolism ... interesting as I say.

The extended family are all well, and expanding - another cousin arrived at the end of January - wonderful to see my little brother Tim and his wonderful wife Betty take the leap into parenthood.

Saskia Ross (Salter) Everything at this end is still pretty much the same as it was last year, except we may finally manage to move house this year if we are very lucky. With India (14) still at Westonbirt, we will not move far. It is lovely to see the school thriving under the brilliant leadership of **Mrs Dangerfield**. Family life is good and all is well, and every time I go to the school, everyone looks extremely cheerful and happy.

Sections 53 and 54 (1983-5)

Section representative:
Sarah Clunie

Sarah Clunie (Roberts) I have been busy with Riding for the Disabled voluntary work recently, now having a local, regional and committee role. Not much time for anything else, though I did manage to have a short holiday to Majorca with a great friend early in the autumn. Our plans for 2015 are massive, and we have decided to move from Winkfield, so the house is on the market at the moment with the hope to sell and move sometime over the summer. We will probably buy a house somewhere further up the Thames Valley. To add to our stress, we have just purchased a boat, which we hope will be moored on the Thames once the restoration work is carried out.

Sections 51 and 52 (1981 and 1982)

Section representative:
Lizzie Mobbs (Overton)
*There is no news from Section 52 this year -
let's hope for a bumper update in the next edition!*

Section 50 (1980)

Section representative:
Lou Walker (Foord)

Antonia Doggart (Ross) Simon and I are still, since 1998, at Caldicott, and somehow still enjoying it. We are looking forward to Simon having two new deputies (pastoral and academic) in the autumn, which will free us up to do so much more than what we are doing at the moment, including overseeing the day-to-day running of the school. Although I have stopped playing netball with the mums, I am still enjoying tennis; walking (last summer I completed the Race to the Stones walk along the Ridgeway) with Monty, our black working cocker spaniel; yoga and pilates; and attending lots of conferences on health, nutrition and general well-being and lifestyle guidance for young people, which I feel is so important in this current work climate. **Griselda Halling (Blood-Smyth)** has been a great help in the past with her school nutritional audits and advice! Clare is about to finish her Marketing and Management degree at Oxford Brookes and is heading for a career in retailing and marketing career. Charlie is loving Newcastle and Sociology, and James, as I write, is in the Amazon as part of his South America gap year travels before going to Edinburgh and Politics and Philosophy. I have been a mean mum and made all of them work and earn money in the holidays in the hope that they may develop a work ethic. I am hoping that many of us in our year may catch up in the summer with **Kate Marchbank** who is coming over from Australia to live in the UK and **Catherine Zuill (aka Bermuda)** who will also be visiting. Many of our year group have been in contact via Facebook since we had our reunion in Oxford a few years ago. It is great to keep in touch!

Tanya Hart (Gee) Tanya has moved to Washington with husband Shep, daughter Gabby (17) and Harry (14).

Kate Marchbank Kate has moved back to London after many years in Australia. She's getting married again and is blissfully happy. She's dreading the British weather though. Her daughter Georgia (19) is at university in Australia. Her son Angus (23) is working at Sony Music in Australia after graduating in December. Both will be over for the wedding in May. She and her husband-to-be Simon plan to move back to Australia eventually, but for a while they'll be settling back here.

Lou Walker (Foord) I'm still a sports massage therapist and athletics coach with a Winchester club. Simon and I are enjoying being empty nesters. Jack (20) is in his second year doing engineering at Leeds, and Charlie (18) is having a gap year before going to university somewhere – she hasn't decided where yet – to do English. She's currently living in Paris, studying French at the Sorbonne. I'm spending more and more time swimming year-round in open water and have entered some really nasty events for this year in preparation for swimming the Straits of Gibraltar next year.

Section 49 (1979)
Section representative:
Fiona Merritt

Olufunso Adegbola (Ige) I've just returned from the US for an education conference in Boston followed by a mini vacation in Atlanta and Houston. I was also in the UK last year and visited Westonbirt for Speech Day with my daughter and cousin and WB classmate, **Morenike (Morohundiya)**. It was such a beautiful day full of reminiscences, as it was the first time either of us had been to WB since we left in 1979!

It was great going round the school premises, classrooms, music rooms, hall, Italian gardens, chapel and grounds with my daughter and meeting current staff, students and parents. It was heartwarming to hear that the current head girl, Subomi Ajibola, is Nigerian! I took pictures in the renovated Holford dorms and my favourite place, the Library. I hope my daughter will be inspired to send her own daughter there.

I am also hoping that we can establish some staff and student exchange and collaboration between WB and my own school, The Vale College, Ibadan, here in Nigeria. My daughter graduated with a Law degree (2.1), from the University of Kent last July and is now at the Nigerian Law School.

As both daughter and son are back in Nigeria now, I won't get to frequent the UK as much as whilst they studied in England, but we are happy the days of overseas student fees are over. Now to preparing for the next generation! Please contact me whenever any of you are in Nigeria. God bless you all.

Mary Ashworth (Moriarty) I guess a few changes going on round here! With two daughters mostly not at home (one married and in Edinburgh, one at university in Leeds), I am now outnumbered by men in my home by three to one! It's okay! My husband Rob had a complete change of jobs last year - out of IT project management into working mainly for a Christian charity that is closely associated with a church in central London, doing all sorts of different things. He still keeps his hand in with IT work, but on a much smaller scale, and I am trying my hand at some new things, as well as helping to look after my aging mother.

We had a rather drastic event in December, which has shaken our world somewhat, when Rob's parents both died suddenly and unexpectedly four days apart. They had just returned from a month in Spain, where they had honeymooned 57 years before and had a very poignant joint funeral a week before Christmas. Consequently, we spent most of December in Devon, with the consolation of their home's splendid sea views and we will be there quite a lot this year as we work our way through the shock and loss and all that goes with it. Suddenly, we are the grownups!

Cheng Sim Chan Limited news to report - still working for a local insurance company and getting older but not much else.

Neelam Christie (Gunther) Happy to report that all is well. Still working in general practice and have just been offered a similar post for less hours and more pay, which I have of course accepted. Recently returned from annual ski trip to France - curate's egg applies, so think I'll have to go earlier for better snow!

Seonaid Coreth (Goodbody) Keeping busy but really nothing new or interesting to report.

Janet Forbes It's been another hectic year. I am still in Nairobi, chugging along at work, and with my new house almost ready to move into, only a year and a half behind schedule! Over the past few years there seems to have been something dramatic to report healthwise every year. This year is no exception, sadly, as the main event of the past year has been the diagnosis of a brain tumour (not malignant, thankfully, but still no fun at all), for which the UN eventually organised a medical evacuation to Sheffield in November for it to be zapped with stereotactic radiosurgery using 201 gamma rays. It was an amazing experience, although in an ideal world I wouldn't need to know that, and hopefully over the next two years or so it will stop the tumour growing. It's still very early days, but the signs so far aren't too worrying, and I'm doing my best to keep going as if everything were normal. So another year, another medical update! Hopefully that really will be it for health hassles for a good while!

Otherwise, I'm busy at work and grabbing the opportunity to explore Kenya and nearby countries whenever possible, including an amazing trip to the Victoria Falls last summer, during which I took a micro-light flight over the Falls and the surrounding Zambian and Zimbabwean countryside, the most terrifying and exhilarating experience of my life!

Joanna Kidson (Rowson) Main focus for 2014 was Bex's final year in school where she almost did everything: House Leader, Peer Support for a group of Year 9s, modelling on the runway in the College fashion show, taking part in Stage Challenge (a student run dance performance), sitting on the Ball and Magazine committees, chairing the Hauora (Spirit) week committee, and choreographing the Year 13 performance for Prize Giving. She continued playing her flute in the Taupo Youth Wind Band as well as her college Stage Band and completed all the requirements for Queen's Guide Award as a Ranger. Despite all this, she also managed to be awarded Dux for her College, a prize for the top academic student of the year, which came complete with a couple of scholarship offers for Universities, but sadly not from the one she had set her heart on! All in all a good year, and one that made her parents very proud!

The rest of us muddled along as usual. I continue to fill my days with being our church treasurer, helping out at one of the local charity shops, helping the librarian at the college, and the occasional bit of book work for clients! Philip keeps the lights burning and the money coming in, Jono and Bex help me spend it.

Philip's parents hit a speed bump health-wise in the middle of the year, which has resulted in them both moving to a rest home and retirement complex just round the corner from us. We fill in the gaps for cooking and shopping as required. With Bex at University we now have two spare rooms and a caravan for anyone visiting the area.

Joan Lowton (Mullens) We had a fabulous year last year, finishing our stint in New Zealand in May, then travelling all around the place: some time in Australia, then to South America, up through the US, mostly to various national parks, including the Grand Canyon, Yellowstone, Zion and Bryce. Then we went up to Alaska for three weeks which was fantastic, followed by three weeks travelling across Canada visiting friends. We had three weeks in the UK, whilst I got a new passport (!), and we got our Indian visas then headed off to south east Asia and India. We arrived back in the UK at the end of December, and I started work again on 12th January. I'm now working in Melton Mowbray instead of Market Harborough, which is a bit of a pain as it is too far to bike to work now. We're back into our house and life continues as if we had never left!

Philippa Meikle (Main) Ticking along but nothing really to report.

Fiona Merritt Mid-2014 saw "bucket list" diving trip to the Galapagos – timing planned for whalesharks, but unfortunately they were late so only one baby seen. Lots of other memorable sights and experiences though. Downhill afterwards as job of nine years died, and I had the joys of trying to persuade someone else I was employable. Getting to grips with terminology of new job and hope will suit.

Better downhill with good week's skiing in Austria in January, and good recent Red Sea week with the dive club, where I managed to win trip awards for both shivering and heat rash, a talent I did not know I had. Specials still feature significantly, especially if include kept-up gym sessions to help pass the now annual fitness test!

Marion Minton I returned from working overseas three and a half years ago, and have had a couple of ups and downs settling back in. I now have a position as a senior teacher for English to overseas students in Bournemouth and am enjoying using smartboards and technology in teaching, very different to the old chalk and blackboards we endured at Westonbirt!

Andrea Radman (Beattie) Recently in Kerala in India on holiday for two weeks' yoga with my own teacher and friends, and then five days chill-out time. I was made redundant beforehand, so back to the UK to find a job or something. I am also part-way through studying to be a yoga teacher with a yoga campus in London - should finish next January, fingers crossed! I've taken the opportunity of apprenticing myself to my own teacher while I am not so busy.

Nikki Tehel (Palmer) Went to the London Christmas Carol Concert put on by the School in December. It was great - the Head and staff are SO lovely. I continue doing PAT (pets as therapy) visits, teaching yoga to adults with learning difficulties (*www.windsoryogatherapy.com*) and some property management and letting. We're still in Windsor but hope to move to Dartmouth. We've had an offer on our house so fingers crossed!

Marguerite Williams (Morris) Have survived my first full busy season at EY. The more I learn the more I seem to find out how little I know. I have just received my CPA general licence from the State of California, so now have a certificate, letters and a number for all those years of studying. I also passed my CISA exam, but that needs another two years of experience before I can claim a licence. There has also been a fair amount of travelling, including three weeks in Seattle, where I managed to have sushi one night with **Tanya Gee**.

Helen is currently job-hunting as she graduates from Edinburgh University this summer with a degree in Infomatics. David is now in his second year at CalPoly in San Luis Obispo, studying Software Engineering. Both Jock and I seem to have spent the last year keeping a closer eye on our mothers, made harder by them being on a different continent.

My mother, **Anne Morris**, had a trip to hospital last March. I was able to fly over and be with her for two weeks. She seems to have recovered but has stopped driving. We were also over for Christmas, when she promptly went down with flu, just about recovering when I left. Jock was in the UK with his mother for much of the autumn. She has now turned 90 and had to be moved into an assisted living facility.

Section 48 (1978)
Section representative:
Amiel Price

Charlotte Harvey (Edgar) Life has taken quite a shift this year. We are officially a childfree zone at home, if you include those at university (3) with our eldest taking up a job in the City. Visits home are pretty regular (thankfully) and always with lots of young, so our house still feels buzzy. Steve continues to work extremely hard developing business projects in America more than the UK. He travels monthly to the States and is currently talking with universities in California, Washington and developing current links with those in New York and Boston.

I have given up teaching after 15 wonderful years at the Steiner School in Forest Row and am involved in two social venture enterprises. One is a local theatre group that brings innovative and challenging productions to the local area, often performing in unusual places, a disused dairy being one! Do come to our shows and look at the website: *www.barebonesproject.co.uk.*

The other project is one I have set up with two friends. Called Bridging Ages, we are keen to link adolescents with the elderly and have started our first project with 16/17 year olds. They are paired up with a local elderly resident and visit weekly listening to their stories. These are written up in the first person, and then we will be publishing them as a memento for the elderly people. It has been a real joy to see the relationships building and the shared pleasure that each group is gaining from this experience.

My new life has given me a greater degree of flexibility of time, very useful as I am now spending more time looking after my mum who is about to undergo a hip replacement - walking currently is almost impossible. I have seen **Joanna Melhuish (Marchbank)** regularly over the year and catch up a little with **Zena Lunn (Marchington)** on Facebook.

Jane John (Thomas) I became Chairman of the Lady Taverners charity in Cardiff and the Vale in October. I still work part-time on a What's On magazine. I am also involved in organising a charity cricket match in aid of the Tom Maynard Trust. My son had a first at uni and is now working as a graduate surveyor in London. My daughter bought a house and is working in PR in Cardiff. I am being bullied into taking up golf but have had a shoulder operation and so that will not be for a while. We had a great year celebrating both parents reaching 80 last year and feel very lucky they are both in good health.

Susan Kennedy (Sheard) The last year has presented its trials and tribulations. I was diagnosed with breast cancer following a routine mammogram at the end of October. Three weeks later I was having a masectomy as there were two tumours in different places and although they were not very big it meant the full op. Unfortunately the three lymph nodes they took at the same time showed cancer in two, much to everyone's surprise, so I then four weeks later had to have another op to remove the remaining 18 lymph nodes. Have been back at work a while now and also managed to get back to running - have got a 10km in March (will go nice and slow). The lymph op was not very nice, and my arm has taken a long time to recover - the anti-cancer drugs don't help that. If you are interested, I have written a blog about the whole thing *(susankadifferentmarathon@wordpress.com)*, to share the story and make it more "normal" especially for our children. Out of a group of five friends my son walked to school with, three of the mums have been diagnosed in the last year, so it's everywhere, and I personally don't think enough people talk about it. (I do also respect those who don't want to talk about it of course).

In other more jolly news my husband Gordon, having finished in the amazing *James Plays* at the National last year, has just started rehearsals for *The Audience* with Kristin Scott Thomas at the Apollo Theatre. Our eldest, James, graduated last summer from Sussex with a First in Economics and is now working in Digital Advertising at Starcom Mediavest. Our youngest, Patrick, is in his second year at Bristol University studying Maths and Philosophy and playing in the American Football team in Defence. So not all bad. Wishing everyone well.

Joanna Melhuish (Marchbank) Not much news. My sister **Kate Marchbank** is remarrying a Brit in May, so I am seeing more of her which is fab. I see **Charlotte Harvey (Edgar)** regularly, and both families still manage to get away with seven out of eight and sometimes eight out of eight kids (this January) even though the oldest are 26 this year! Long may it continue - their partners will bump up the numbers though.

Amiel Price I seem to have had lots of visitors since moving to my new home in Langland. It overlooks both sea and golf course, which has been delightful (both the visitors and the views). **Alicia Holmes (Rolston)** and her husband came to stay the very first night I moved in. They didn't seem to mind the chaos as they'd been camping and were quite glad of a decent bed and a washing machine. Alicia is a part-time chaplain in a care home and is also busy with church outreach work. Her son had a nasty traffic accident in London whilst on a bike but is recovering well, and her daughter is working with the homeless in Leeds: "She rings up with dire stories of her homeless but always seems to find a silver lining."

Since December I have been retired from the BBC (obviously very early!) so that I can spend more time with Dad and concentrate on emptying a family home full of generations of stuff. I have never been busier and I haven't quite worked out how to allow time for a walk on the Gower. It's ridiculous! Dad is recovering from his second cataract operation but he is definitely slower in the winter months, so we're hoping a sunny warm spring might perk him up a bit. Mike is dividing his time between here and his home and being very supportive. I have seen a lot of **Charlotte Walpole**. We enjoyed a lovely holiday in Brittany last year, and earlier celebrated her daughter gaining a distinction for her MA.

I also hear from **Amelia Trevethick** who took redundancy in December and is job hunting, unless she's already found one that is. And **Sallie Robertson (Rowson)** keeps in touch too. She and Fraser were off to visit her sister **Jo Rowson** in New Zealand at the end of January.

Their children: Duncan is being an architect in Bath, Guy is in his final year at Surrey, and Bryony is working to save money for pre-university travels. I also heard from **Jane Tompsett (Hunter)** whose daughter is now at York University. Jane is involved with her local church, has an internet business and keeps in touch with **Sue McCarthy**.

Lorraine Stanton (Martin) Mark and I decided we were running out of steam, and so we have put our farm up for sale and sold all our beautiful animals. It's a sad time, but now I do have chance to spend time with our daughters, Anna, who has one daughter and another on the way, and Emily, who is getting married this year. What I will do with my days I'm not yet sure, although I'm very clear I'm unlikely to be sitting and twiddling my thumbs! *(See also Lorraine's catering website: www.OurFarmhouseKitchen.co.uk)*

Liz White I'm well and seem to be as busy as ever work and hobby wise. Having moved back to Andover last year to work for Army HQ and cut back my travelling time considerably, I still managed to find myself a busy job, programme-managing the development of a data warehouse and trying to bring some data coherence to the Army, a job which quite frankly will last me well past my retirement age!

I'm still very active with my tennis club in Salisbury having taken on the rather onerous (at this time of year) job of match secretary as well as playing in three teams and captaining at least one of those. Some things just never change. To stop me getting a moment's rest, my brothers have given me a Mirror dinghy which my nephews no longer want, and the plan is to join a sailing club in the Solent, which should be good fun and create a lot of general entertainment!

My partner and I plus dog, visited Westonbirt Arboretum last autumn and, wow, what a commercial venture it's become, rather too managed for my liking, but at least being appreciated by many. Trips this year look to be sport-focussed, with Six Nations Rugby and Davis Cup tennis already experienced so bring on Wimbledon, Eastbourne and the Rugby World Cup.

Stephanie Wolfe (Binder) Still running a garden maintenance business and not getting rich doing it, but great job satisfaction, My mother died very suddenly last July, so with my sister **Jenny** we have been doing our best to support my father who was badly hit after over 50 years of marriage.

My youngest is now at university reading archeaology at Cardiff. We went down for the weekend a little while ago and were struck by the sheer number of hen and stag parties going there. Maybe Prague has finally got too expensive?! I did enjoy the Dr Who Experience - a real trip down memory lane.

During the summer we hand-reared a duckling abandoned by his mother and who imprinted herself on me. She lives in a specially constructed duck house in the garden and was joined by Dulcie who was being severely bullied by the hens. Duckling loves to hop inside at every opportunity and greet Simon's notary clients. After being made redundant, Simon has found employment 3 days a week at a firm in Gravesend and does his notary work on the other two days as well as keeping bees.

I am still being a Lay Minister locally, taking school assemblies, services and generally trying to keep everything going in the small rural parishes. We have the usual problems of ancient buildings, huge insurance costs, small congregations and huge parish shares to pay. Every year I suggest closing the church and meeting in the Village Hall instead, and this year for the first time people actually started to look quite thoughtful! All the other three children are now mostly gainfully employed and require only the occasional handout and laundry service!

Section 47 (1977)
Section representative:
Fiona Leith

Sue Brough (Purnell) I have had two tough years on the personal front but hopefully on the way up now. Joshua, my son, has set up his own business as a property developer and is doing well. Kate, my daughter, has started a business studies course and absolutely loving it. Just about to take her driving test too. Mum (85) is living with us and is truly amazing. Still working for Help the Aged! I am working hard in HR and been heavily involved in new acquisitions and bids for a private equity company. Have spent a few months in India setting up a new office which has been an incredible experience. Still playing in a local orchestra and regularly perform solos at concerts. Few more wrinkles each year and a few more pounds but enjoying life.

Fiona Dix (Bolus) In 2014, I found my life turning almost full circle! My daughter, Charlotte (12) started Lower 4 at St Swithun's School, Winchester in September last year. This is notable for its connection to my previous life at Westonbirt. Readers of Section 47 in particular will doubtless remember my passion not only for lacrosse, in particular, but for every sport, including Junior Dancing - who remembers that on a Saturday night? - and I am delighted to report that St Swithun's School will attend the major end-of-year lacrosse tournament which is being held at Westonbirt in May 2015. How I shall enjoy and reminisce whilst standing on the sidelines watching my 'chip off the old block' tear up and down the field! People say that we even look similar!

Otherwise, I am really busy doing as much as possible for my local community via the Parish Council. In particular I am leading a project to bring traffic calming to our little village which is torn in half by the dreaded A272 trunk road. When implemented, our scheme will be the first such road project in the South Downs National Park, so there is a lot of expectation riding on it. Riding too plays a big part in life.

We have just bought Charlotte's first horse: she says she wants to be a world-class event rider. I might be allowed to hang on her coat tails as groom, which secretly I would love as I really enjoy being near horses.

My son, Monty (14), at Canford School in Dorset is keeping us busy round the country, taking him to play in real tennis events. This is his chosen sport and great love. There are so few courts to play on in the country that there is always a lot of travelling. It is great to see him so involved in something he is passionate about.

Beyond that, what precious little time is left is spent tending to the wonderful spring garden we inherited when we moved here. It should be open to the public but I am not quite brave enough yet. That's one for the future.

Katherine Hill (Cemlyn-Jones) This year Richard and I officially reached the season of the empty nest, although the reality has been that the house is still full most weekends! I am enjoying my role as UK Director for the national charity Care for the Family (*www.careforthefamiy.org.uk)*, which as well as being on the leadership team involves speaking, writing and travelling (and a lot of Premier Inns!)

We have a fun and busy year ahead with two weddings: George, our eldest, is marrying Ellie in July, and then our daughter Charlotte is marrying her fiancé, Will, in September. Like the buses they come together. I was invited to speak at a Westonbirt church service at the end of last year, followed by coffee in the hall - a real trip down memory lane.

Cherry James (Lucas) Oh dear, news much the same as usual! Still working as a law lecturer; still living in Vauxhall; still enjoying singing and travelling (not generally at the same time). Husband Simon still working as a solicitor; son Freddie just about to start a two-year postgraduate organ course at Stuttgart Music School (which will give us welcome opportunities to see **Nicky Volkommer (Sperry)** again as she lives near Stuttgart); Anna is back at Durham after her year abroad in Germany and France; she is now heading towards finals this summer. I enjoy seeing both **Henrietta Ewart** and **Corinna Kershaw (Chown)** quite regularly.

Serena Jones (Walthall) Having done 10 years as Editor of this News, I have now handed over to Debbie Young, who has experience in publishing and has great ideas for bringing it into the 21st century. I'm sure you will notice some changes when this edition is printed! Thank you so much, Debbie, for taking it on.

My usual activities now involve volunteering, fitness, bridge and singing (now in a chamber choir as well as a choir and quartet). I have just started a woodworking course, for which the first project is to make a bookcase using three different types of joint, all done by hand. My first session was this week, and I can see it's going to be a long road!

I am keeping in touch with Guide Dogs and hope to 'board' some puppies this year when their puppy-walkers are away. The puppy we trained has become a successful guider with a blind lady in Leicestershire but it broke our hearts when she left us. We're still in touch with her, though, and visit occasionally.

Kim is in her first year at Nottingham Trent University, doing Law. She's happy with both her choice of university and course, which is a relief. Vanessa is in her first year of A Levels at the local school and enjoying life (yes, that means the work is secondary!)

I went to the Westonbirt Carol Service in London with **Mary Wickenden** and **Wendy McWilliams** and about 60 other old girls. We had a good sing-song and catch-up. The three of us had a meal out afterwards, and I stayed the night with Mary. It was good to have an event in London as it attracted some different people, and hopefully it will be repeated this year.

Sally Kincaid (Franklin) I have always loved the concept of the 'forever' family home. A place to set down roots, bring up the family and have them return in due course with grandchildren etc etc. Clearly that is a life for someone else. We seem to have led a ridiculously peripatetic existence that saw us move into our 11th family home a few months ago. Why? Don't know really - just because...

We now live (for how long I wonder) at a place called Mount Macedon. It's about 60km north of Melbourne and best known for its large homes, spectacular gardens, and cooler climate than the city. We inherited a once significant but somewhat neglected garden, which has required a great deal of work, and will do for quite a while - a large walled vegetable garden which is my particular domain - and a number of rare and exotic plants. All this rather monopolises the weekends unfortunately though it is something both Andrew and I enjoy.

Andrew continues as a Member at the Victorian Civil and Administrative Tribunal (VCAT), alternating days sitting as "Judge Judy" with somewhat heavier duty cases. He loves the case mix and face-to-face dealings with the public, but was a bit shocked at first to find that he 'only' had 20 days annual leave per annum, having had as much as he liked when at the Bar, and plenty of occasional holidays when in Oman. Welcome to the real world, I say.

I continue on in general practice land as CEO of a not-for-profit company called GPRA, working with medical students, junior doctors and general practice registrars. In a perfect world, I would like to reduce my days here to four a week, but I can't see that happening in the near future. Currently there's lots of travelling involved, and there is rarely a week when I don't have to jump on a plane somewhere which becomes pretty disruptive. However, I love the job, so disruption and no four-day week is just something I have to suck up and wear.

Jack is in his third year at University and has also been accepted into a part time NIDA (Australian version of RADA) course. He spent the summer doing an internship with the Melbourne Theatre Company working on the pre-production of the Australian adaptation of "Jumpy" and loved it. This has rather cemented his ideas regarding his future career, and he is now talking about auditioning for full time NIDA or RADA when he graduates. Looks like we may be supporting him for quite some time, but if he takes the RADA route, then I have excellent excuses for more regular trips to the northern hemisphere!

By the time this goes to print I will probably have been back to the UK (first few weeks of April), and so hopefully will have caught up with some of the Section 47 group. I'm having a few days in Turkey with my sister and brother-in-law, then a few days in London, Shropshire and possibly Pembrokeshire. My planned UK visit last November (2014) had to be cancelled late in the piece so I am really looking forward to this trip.

Ruby Lau Still around and extremely busy in India (Chennai) mostly and China and Singapore as a Consultant on AMI Montessori Training courses and schools. Exam time approaching! Being back in Asia gives me the opportunity of visiting my mum in Malaysia more often and more easily. I am in the UK for short periods, a few times a year. Hoping one of the visits will coincide with get-togethers one of these years.

Fiona Leith (Goodbody) I am still helping to run our family farm near Inverness and locally here am doing the usual round of charity fundraising. A friend and I held our second plant sale in 2014, which was very successful, but the time taken in raising the plants meant the garden ran away in the spring and I never quite caught up. This year we have decided to open my garden to the public and sell fewer plants in a bid to at least have the garden looking nice for the summer and not too much of a jungle. **Susie Younger (Goodbody, Section 49)** and I walked the first part of the Pennine Way in July. It was surprisingly empty and really quite a challenge. Luckily we are both prone to similar aches and pains, so make good walking companions!

I am hoping to complete the Pennine Way this year. I have just become a governor of our local primary school, which already looks like an interesting challenge. Charlie is still doing classic car brokerage and one of our sons is equally interested in old cars. He has just bought himself a 1924 Austin 7 Chummy and now drives everywhere in it, when not fettling it. Our lives are fairly dominated by old cars, both for work and pleasure - even I have a 1967 Alfa Spider (think "The Graduate") which I swan around in during the summer.

I had a very nice surprise a few months ago, on arriving home, to find **Fiona Dix (Bolus)** parked in the drive. She had been delivering a horse somewhere locally and had a few minutes to spare. It was lovely to catch up.

Wendy McWilliams This has been a difficult year. My ex was tragically involved in a serious car accident just before Christmas and air lifted to John Radclifffe in Oxford, but his injuries were so severe that he died in the New Year. A massive shock and loss for my children, and, despite twelve years of an acrimonious and difficult divorce, it left me with very mixed feelings.

Kids are coping well and more than capable of maximum manipulation in a weak moment and talked me into getting two cocker spaniel puppies - how did I fall for that?! They are cute and adorable but very far from housetrained, have had two emergency trips to the vet, eaten my new sofa, eat all paper and mats laid down for the mucky business, so have shredded paper to deal with too. I have also had to organise puppy day care at vast expense, just like recruiting nannies all over again. Also have to deal with securing pet passports, microchips, insurance and rabies jabs so they can come to France with us in the summer. However, they are doing the job they were recruited to do and kids no longer come home to an empty house, and it is quite difficult to sustain sadness when being mobbed by mad, bouncy, squeaky fur balls.

Harry just departed for five weeks in Mexico and Cuba, on a couple of days' notice, but is then coming back to re-sit an English A Level and hopefully lift it to secure the university of his choice - UCL or Leeds. Emma and Lucy coming up to AS exams so another few months of high stress and drama, but looking forward to the final year of school fees. Still working hard with long hours, but beginning to think retirement, which always felt like it happens to others, is a possibility, but not for a good few years yet. Hoping to travel to California in the summer (without the puppies) to see my brother and family. Good luck to all.

Tina Panton (Galanis) Finally completed the purchase of our new home in Greece last July, not a minute too soon, as our first guests arrived in June and the last didn't leave until the end of October! The builders have now installed themselves. We're hoping for a whirlwind of activity between now and April, otherwise it will be another summer of camping! I'm enjoying winter in Symi. The weather was wonderful up till Christmas; I was still swimming mid-December. January has made up for it by being unseasonably cold, wet and windy. Marooned here at the moment, gale-force winds have caused all boats to be cancelled. It could be days, so stocked up on food yesterday - yes, the shops do run out! Luckily I'm alone (with the cats), so I don't have to put up with the husband and kids moaning about the lack of facilities, I can just please myself - doing a lot of reading and very little housework! Happy days.

Catherine Porter (Bullock) Life continues much as before here in Stirling. I am still teaching locally and currently again teach all the classes from P1–P7 during the week. I am still (amongst other things) teaching French, which I love, and cover non-class-contact time for other staff in the school. My youngest is now 21, and other children are 24, 30 and 32, so I feel increasingly old! However, that said, my dear Mum **(Mrs Bullock, Staff)** is still going strong and is now 95! We go down to Gloucestershire to see her as often as we can, and whilst there over the summer, it was great to catch up with **Corinna Kershaw (Chown)**. It was a very long time indeed since we had met, but it was wonderful to see her again and she met Mum again too. A fabulous day was had by all! As always we would welcome any of our section who venture North, so let me know if you are ever in the area! All the best to one and all.

Katherine Pratt Still based in Kent and enjoying working three days a week as a home worker. This arrangement means I can visit our offices in Canary Wharf/Waterloo, work from my boyfriend's house in Devon or my parents' house in Hampshire if required. In 2014 I helped my parents, now in their late 80s and early 90s, move to a chalet-bungalow close to their old home. Then I spent most of last summer down in Devon with David, where I did quite a bit of painting. In August we started to build a 'stick and glue' sailing/rowing boat and look forward to using it to explore the shallow rivers/creeks of Devon.

Leigh Ralphs (Davidson) This year has gone by in a flash! My mother arrived to stay with us from Spain with her first attack of gout and hasn't gone back! She is nearly 94 and has vascular dementia so we take each day as it comes.

I have been working all hours as Project Co-ordinator for Malvern College's 150th Anniversary. We have about 40 events organised which is pretty ambitious. We kicked off with the opening of the new Razak Science Centre by the Prime Minister of Malaysia (OM), a Thanksgiving Service in the local Priory with the Bishop and various exhibitions, musical masterclasses, lectures and sporting fixtures. I am looking forward to a 150th Dinner at the House of Lords next weekend and we go out with a bang with a celebratory Ball in July by which time I will need a long holiday!

We had a wonderful holiday to St Lucia last Easter (my first helicopter ride!) and a trip to Spain with friends in July. Charlie and James travelled around Cambodia, Vietnam and Thailand over the summer.

Charlie is still at Gordon's School and James has started at Bryanston. Both love teaching (Maths and Geography) and manage to continue to play hockey as well. We had a lovely graduation day with James at Bath Abbey last summer.

As Secretary of the Westonbirt Association, I get to see more of **Serena Jones (Walthall)** and **Jenny Webb (Binder)** which is a great treat, and **Fiona Dix (Bolus)** popped in to see us when they were staying locally. My goddaughter Charlotte Hill, daughter of **Katherine Hill (Cemlyn-Jones)**, is getting married in September, so I am really looking forward to catching up with Twitter then! The Association had a great day out at Highgrove (my first time there) but sadly I missed the WB Carol Concert in London as I was at a wedding. I hope they will repeat it next year.

I have started to have golf lessons which seems to be better for my back than tennis (sadly) but am definitely going to be a fair weather player only! We're still walking the Malvern Hills when we have time, and Guyon is enjoying life at Malvern. He has been to China to help with the setting up a new school and we both went to Cairo for an amazing celebration of the start of a partnership with a new school there - the highlight was seeing the pyramids for the first time!

Penny Sloman (Sheard) Just to say my family are all good. Sam, our middle son has gone to join the Swire Group in the Far East and is living in China. We went to visit him in Xiamen in November. Ollie is still working as a structural engineer in London and Nick is at Edinburgh. I am ladies' captain at my local tennis club, and one of the highlights of my tennis career has been playing at Wimbledon a couple of times in recent weeks. I enjoyed the baths and members' dining room. I am planning to work at Wimbledon for three weeks this summer, before going to Japan to meet up with all the children. Horry is still a partner at Accenture and working on the Future of Work.

Nicola Volkommer (Sperry) It's been a year of major family milestones. Our son Daniel married his girlfriend of many years, Linda, in a moving ceremony in November. (Three down, one to go!)

Before that, we became doting grandparents of Debbie and Alex's baby daughter, Lucia Aurelia, and discovered that our capacity for drooling over babies is alive and well, even after all these years. They lived with us during Debbie's baby break, but they are now back in Berlin. Debbie has picked up her work at the Foreign Office again, as Protocol Officer and Diplomat, organizing Chancellor Angela Merkel's foreign tours and meeting foreign Heads of State and Royalty, while Alex is taking paternal leave.

Stefan and Johanna are settled nearby, and Jessica is following my footsteps in Cambridge, enjoying a year at Lucy Cavendish College and experiencing the adrenalin of getting essays done on time for supervisions. We miss having a house full of children, but enjoying the novelty of tidying up and finding it still tidy after half an hour!

My first novel is about to be published, and my life revolves more and more around books and the pitfalls of the publishing scene. It's a whole new world, especially doing it all in a foreign language. I still feel a novice, having never aspired to becoming an author, let alone expected it, but gingerly testing whether it's something to build on for the future. My book on raising children (nothing very fancy or professional - just honest, funny anecdotes about chaotic days with four small children) has gone into its third edition, and new ideas keep coming.

Teaching and church fill up the rest of the time, and we're grateful for another year of good health, great kids and kids-in-law, and the privilege of living in a peaceful country in times in which this can no longer be taken for granted.

Jennifer Webb (Binder) It has been a very difficult year. My mother died unexpectedly, and we were so close that the shock and grieving and supporting my father really used up a lot of emotional and physical energy. We had a few hiccups with boys in their respective lives so they also needed time and support. Sometimes you go on being a parent for longer than you might imagine! Throw in my Governor and Westonbirt responsibilities, not to mention various other 'good works' (so I won't), and there has not been much time for fun. However, before all that happened, John and I celebrated our 25th wedding anniversary in Crete, which we loved, and I am still playing tennis, bridge and walking.

Mary Wickenden Another busy year for me. I am still teaching and doing research at UCL about disability, mainly in developing countries. At the moment, I'm very taken up with a project in Malawi and Uganda, which is interesting and challenging and I'm learning a lot! I travel to both countries every few months, and usually it's all quite busy and not much playtime. However in November I managed to tack on a great holiday driving around Malawi with a friend. If you have never seen really, really big potholes, this is the place to try them! Beautiful country too! Otherwise still enjoying London and also doing all the usual outdoorsy things but seem to have increasingly creaky joints. Trying to remember however that 'if you rest you rust!'

Section 46 (1976)
Section representative:
Jean Stone

Jane Baker (Vass) I am head of public policy at Age UK, the UK's largest charity working to improve later life. Homewise I have a grown up son and a student daughter, and my husband Ian and I live near High Wycombe.

Gillian Marriott (Gillett) I'm in the middle of packing up some of the house (should be packing for holiday to India next week) as after 21 years in this lovely old townhouse it's badly in need of some tlc - pointing, new windows, boiler, radiators, sitting room being gutted etc - dust everywhere.

Boys on half term - it's the last few months of school holidays for us. Hopefully Patrick (18) will get the grades he needs for York and David (20) leaves college in July with an uncertain future ahead of him.

Having started boot camp (who would have thought!) in 2013 the Sunday morning classes ended last summer, but I still continue various exercise classes in the week - continual battle with weight. I even went to a few boxing sessions, but it meant being up before 6 am and was around the time my father passed away, and I couldn't commit to twice weekly sessions, but I loved it!

Love living in Chipping Norton, always something going on and great selections of foodie places nearby too. Enjoy volunteering at local events especially ChipLitFest held in April, where I'm normally selling books on behalf of our fab local bookshop. Annual holidays to the Scillies still the highlight of my year, and last year took Mum and a carer for a week in May as well - any excuse to visit! Also had a couple of long weekends in Italy, which were great fun. Still in touch with **Sue (Spud)** but don't get to see her often enough though.

Margaret Metcalfe (Haviland) I am still Health Visiting in Southampton, after having a rush of blood to the head a couple of years ago when I defected from community midwifery in Salisbury to do the full time HV course. It is great actually, and I am enjoying the broader scope of work and the regular hours. However, four days leaves little time for being organised. I am also topping up the PGDip I got with the course with a dissertation (it's only an essay!) to make it an MSc, and the deadline for the proposal to be submitted is in two days. Family are all well. My sisters are thriving. I am going to visit Angie in USA next month, and I see Jane a fair bit. My father celebrated his 90th birthday last April and is still very fit, thank goodness. I have seen **Anna (Worlidge)** recently and **Mary-Jane Isaac** within the last year. **Mandy Evans (Morgan)** is hoping to visit soon and I also hope to get to see **Nicky Capewell (Wilson)** to reminisce on our gap year all those years ago!"

Helen Owens (Kucharek) My only news is that I'm still teaching singing at Westonbirt! My husband has recently been ordained as a Pastor (which makes me a Pastor's wife, I guess!) and we are responsible for a church campus which meets in a cinema in Hengrove, Bristol. We are a part of Carmel City Church - one church, many locations.

Clare Savoca After my father's death in August 2012, I spent the next 16 months wading my way through my father's papers. Added to that, as I found myself kicked out of the family apartment, a fourteen-month search began for a more accessible nest. Cleaning up an apartment with five bedrooms is no piece of cake, especially if both parents were messy pack rats. But all of that is water under the bridge.

In December 2013, I moved into the ideal apartment. It is in the area where I grew up and which I love. It has two bedrooms, very spacious, and a beautiful view of the Jet d'eau and the Mont-Blanc. This last year I spent furnishing and beautifying it to my taste. Now my mind is free to get back to my writing.

In late summer, my Aunt and Uncle invited me to Gainesville, Virginia, USA. They hosted a family reunion over three days. It was a wonderfully organized event. We were about 70, some of us had not seen each other for 10, 20, 30 years. We had such great fun!

Jean Stone (Borritt) The last 12 months have passed extremely quickly, but it has been a very happy year. Both my daughters graduated last July. Eleanor is working hard as a junior doctor in Newcastle-upon-Tyne. Aly is an Audiologist at Addenbrookes Hospital in Cambridge but she is also studying part-time for a Masters in Clinical Science from Manchester University. Aly's boyfriend asked me just before her birthday for my permission to ask her to marry him, and consequently we are now planning a wedding for October this year. I am delighted!

Another highlight event was a trip down the zip wire over the Bethesda quarry in Snowdonia. It is nearly a mile long and runs 500 feet above the quarry at its highest point. The harness contraption means that you are whizzing down the wire in a horizontal position at speeds of up to 100 mph. We had a lovely clear day, and I could see over the Menai Straits to Anglesey as I hurtled down. The ride was over in about a minute, but it was exhilarating and brilliant fun – highly recommended.

I have just returned from a week snowshoe walking and hiking in the French Alps, which I tried as a change from skiing. I was certainly able to take in more of the scenery and wildlife, so it was a pleasant change.

Section 45 (1975)
Section representative:
Fiona Stokes (Tobin)

Fiona Stokes (Tobin) Caught up last summer with **Anne Millman**, **Ali Cheeseman (Dorey)** and **Jenefer Greenwood**, at Anne and Hans' new home, beautiful Brook Cottage in Blewbury. We lunched in the local pub and caused consternation amongst the locals with our laughter. Jen is supremely good at mimicry! (Clearly her acting skills from schooldays are still useful.) Also saw **Clare Williams** at Grange Park Opera when for once the weather was kind to us. Had a good catch-up with **Trudy Evans (Wardle)** just before Christmas at a mutual friend's party in Reigate. I meet up periodically with **Lizzie Bennett (Phelps)** in Richmond and keep in touch via email with **Jocelyne Grobler (Clarke)** in South Africa, **Sarah Sladden (Deterding)** in Botswana and **Jane Golding (Gaffney)** in France. Have also briefly seen **Lorna Hooley (Lovell)** and **Jane Seymour**. Great sadnesses recently - went to the funerals of Clare's mother in January and Lizzie's brother in February.

Liz Bennett (Phelps) The last year has flown by. The past couple of months have been a bit of a blur as my brother died in early January. He was only 55. He was diagnosed with a form of motor neurone disease nearly 25 years ago, and more recently his health had slowly been deteriorating. Although it was to be expected, it has still been quite a shock. My father, who will be 89 this year, has found it particularly hard to come to terms with.

Billie Trimble (Barrow Green) We continue to love life back in Somerset. Even managed to find a house next to friendly old girl **Priscilla Boddington**! Izzy (daughter) loving the fast and whizzy advertising world in Covent Garden and Barn is in his final year at York, leaning towards a career in antiquarian books (but how does one live?) or a Masters in Law. Time will tell. Just returned from a visit to Crufts with god-daughter **Clare Hooley** (daughter of **Lorna Lovell**). It is our third visit together and always great fun with non-stop talk!

Gilly Stuart Smith (Ward) The most remarkable event in the Stuart Smith household this year is that Marcus, our eldest, managed to get accepted into Newcastle Uni despite being two grades off his offer! The whole summer had been blighted by his fear of failure,but then his initial despair turned to amazement when he opened his UCAS page and it said 'Congratulations'. He still had to ring the university to check they really meant it! So he is well into his first year reading Chemistry and having a great time. Otherwise life in Sussex is varied – lots of tennis and bridge – and we are planning a trip to Alaska this summer.

Anne Millman I've had a wonderful first year in our new (very ancient) home in the village of Blewbury, South Oxfordshire. The villagers have made us very welcome, and we are so enjoying this beautiful place and discovering long walks over the downs that surround us.

My first ever allotment has been very abundant (with the exception of parsnips and carrots - anyone got any tips?), and our cottage garden is beautiful. I still can't believe it, really. The move has also meant I'm nearer to some of our former class mates, and I've enjoyed catching up with **Jenny Greenwood**, **Fiona Stokes (Tobin)** and **Alison Dore**y who have been here to paddle in the brook beside our house. They also joined a tea party here with **Valerie Byrom Taylor** and my mum. And I've also seen **Trudy Wardle** a couple of times since the move.

My working life continues to be very busy and varied - the current list Tate, the National Trust, Portsmouth D-Day Museum, Hampshire Libraries and several more. So I continue to travel quite a bit, and enjoy the variety very much indeed. If truth be told I would like to be a little less busy workwise, but don't tell anyone. My husband, Hans, has built up his psychotherapy practice very quickly here, so we have absolutely no regrets about leaving London. In fact, we've never looked back.

Clare Williams The good part of the past year is that October saw me celebrating seven years living in Hong Kong, and I am now a Permanent Resident, which means that I can vote, buy an apartment without paying 15% extra duty (not that I can afford to buy anything here) and no longer need to be sponsored for work. At the same time, I changed jobs within Barclays, which has involved quite a transition from leading a team of 11 around the region, to being a one-person band and developing a new regional role.

The really not good part of the past year is that my mother died at Christmas while I was on holiday in Burma, and so I spent January in the UK helping my brothers to sort out all the things that need to be sorted following a death. I was very grateful to **Jane Seymour**, **Fiona Stokes (Tobin)** and **Lorna Hooley** for all their support and friendship during an incredibly difficult period. My father turned 89 in February; we have installed the "Country Cousin" system to look after him which does take some pressure off me, but he is challenged by IT and deaf, so it is very hard to keep in touch with him, other than via good old fashioned letters and postcards. Remember them? Now I write to him on Sunday nights - I feel like I am back at school! I do hope I can get back for whatever 40 years on we manage to organise.

Susie Younger (Goodbody) We have had a shake up this year with Douglas getting a very bad pulmonary embolism (lungs full of blood clots) We have been told it is amazing that he is not dead, but recovery is going to take some time. Luckily we sold our herd of Highland cattle last year given what happened, and I am now trying to persuade him to sell all our other cattle, as we have had to get someone in to help with calving, which is not cost-effective. Also, it would be great to be able to go away for a weekend on the spur of the moment, something we have never been able to do with cows to look after!

I am still getting over the stresses of the referendum and am frankly rather ashamed to be Scottish just now, given how some of our fellow countrymen and women are behaving. It sadly does not seem to be abating, and I think unless it does, a lot of people are going to leave. Unfortunately, it is rather more difficult as a farmer to up sticks quickly if everything goes horribly pear-shaped! Our sons are still gainfully employed, living in London, which is great, but my dream of them coming north to live and work, which they used to want to do, is vanishing, and I don't blame them!

Section 44 (1974)
Section representative:
Elizabeth Battye (Jones)

Tina Cook (Jenne) It was lovely to see everyone who was able to make the reunion last autumn, and so good that Pauline was there, having done the majority of the organising. The new head looks incredibly young, but obviously has lots of great ideas and energy. It was great to have a sunny day and so to be able to wander around all parts of the school and grounds.

Just off to a music conference in London with **Carol Pusey (Cleal),** so it will be good to spend time in a hotel the evening before, catching up.

Life has been sad and busy for us recently as my beloved aunt died last month, and as she had been living with us since Christmas we have felt it even more. There seems to be lots of sorting to do as she cared for so many people during her life. It's very poignant going through other people's belongings.

Hannah continues to enjoy life as a medical student in Leeds, somehow managing to fit in lots of extra-curricular activities as well. I gather that this will have to change in the next year or two however.

An autumn trip to Rome was blessed with sunny weather, so we were able to eat outside during the day at café tables in the sun in spectacular surroundings.

Jenny Denholm (Goodbody) Jenny is now living in Edinburgh Morningside. Her daughters have found a house on one level as Jenny is now confined to a wheelchair. Her eldest daughter Kate is marrying this summer, which is very exciting. She is also composing. Cara is working in HR in London and Glasgow. Seonaid is a cabinet maker (bespoke pieces), and Laura is a surveyor. They all live in London except for Seonaid who is in Edinburgh.

Charlotte England (Wren) It was great to come back to England for the 40th anniversary of leaving WB. It was a very long way from Melbourne however, without doubt, worth the effort. How lovely to see so many faces and to hear how everyone's life had evolved. I couldn't believe how many people came to the day. It was so well run and a big thank you to all who put it together. Westonbirt looked lovely on the day. It made me reflect how important my time there was. The influence on my life has been enormous. It was a real home to me, and the extra-curricular activities that I developed while I was there, particularly in the music area, have been a bonus for life. It was great to see so many happy students and to also go to areas of the school which were out of bounds, particularly other house areas such as dorms. Beaufort definitely didn't get the 'first pick' on those, however we still had a lot of fun! Again thanks to all the organisers of the 40th for a wonderful day.

Julia Goss (Wilcox) It was so good to meet up with so many of you at the October reunion. I am still reeling to think that we all left 40 years ago. Shortly after the reunion, I joined my husband in Saudi Arabia, and I am now getting used to life in this strange country. We are living in a compound in a city in the north of the country. Life in the compound is very pleasant, and there is a nice group of people from all over the world who are very friendly. Life outside is strange and challenging, not least whenever I go out wearing the abaya (the cloak thing - WB's cloak in comparison is a fashion item!) I manage to come back fairly frequently to the UK to see family.

Pauline Jackson (Garrett) It has been a sad year. Henry died whilst we were on holiday in Spain last summer. After a 40 year close partnership, life now is so very different. My family is keeping me busy however - youngest David (23) has moved back home. Laura (26) is studying at the British Film and Television School in Beaconsfield. She took me to see her brother Paul (30) in Colombia for Christmas. Paul is on about his third Gap Year! Stephen (33) is taking me to Florida with his wife and four children at Easter. Maybe some baby-sitting will be in order?! I have several chronic health issues, and I will keep my fingers crossed that I feel up to the Florida holiday.

After 17 years working at the same school, I retired at the end of February.

It was such a pleasure to see so many old faces (not literally!) at our Section's 40 year reunion last October. Friends came from all corners of England, Scotland and Wales, **Elspeth Weaver (Bolus)** from France and **Charlotte England (Wren)** from Australia.

Tish John (Bush) Both of our sons are now married which makes life a bit less hectic, except that the youngest has gone out to Australia for a couple of years. We are going out to see him for a couple of weeks and feel very privileged having never been to Australia! It was fantastic meeting up with so many people last year, and particular thanks to Pauline and Pippa.

Elspeth Weaver (Bolus) I have bought a small house in the town that I've known for ages and where I know a huge amount of people. I still have an enormous amount of work to do on it. I continue to teach in some schools and companies. My boys have all finished their studies. Oliver continues to be an executive farm manager near Tours and has bought a 200-acre farm with his father. Freddy is working in logistics locally for the company which makes pyre, and George has just qualified as an engineer and started working for Continental down in Toulouse.

Section 43 (1973)

Section representative:
Sarah Thomas

Lorraine Clemie (Gibbs) I have taken a couple of years out from Speech and Language Therapy, but have decided to go back and do some work again as I miss the patients so much. John is well and we are both very excited at the prospect of becoming grandparents in August. Alex and Charlotte are thrilled. Jack is with a wonderful girl called Rita and her lovely son Matas. We have now bought some sheep together with some land in Yorkshire. Our first lambs are due on the 28th of this month!

Karen Evans (Edwards) The main event of the last year was her daughter's marriage from home. Karen often sees **Gail Robinson** (who is her daughter's godmother). She also saw **Jane Morgan** recently.

Tish Golding I really enjoyed a visit to WB last October with **Anti Seymour-Williams'** year (Section 44?). A terrific turnout and a lovely reunion. Good to catch up with **Pippa Mason, Helen Prior** and **Charlotte Wren** from Beaufort. Lottie had come all the way from Australia. So many others too - all just great to see again. (See next Section's notes for everyone who came. I think our Section should do something similar soon before we all get too much longer in the tooth.) Good to see all the changes though a twinge of sadness for the departure of the old desks and chests of drawers! What, no more trips to the can room?

Family news: Maddie, our eldest, is doing a fine job with her two little people (6 and 15 months); Harry is about to do his finals at Bristol and Louisa is about to do her A Levels and then, yippee, we'll be free of school terms.

Maurice and I are still working, but happily he is going down to four days from May. I'm still at the BBC. Lots of changes. Nice to see **Sally-Anne Thomas** at one of the many leaving do's the other day. This year have also seen **Carol Kynnersley**, who has also become a grandmother, and **Lorrie Gibbs**. Sorry I can't remember everyone's married names. Great to see them too. And of course **Jean and Sarah Leslie**. Just so sorry it was in such sad circumstances. It made me realise we need to make the most of family and friends.

My mother is still in Sussex, and I visit fairly often though happily she is fairly adventurous about getting on with her life now she is on her own. Otherwise life ploughs on as hectic as ever, which is good.

Rekha Ghose She is still working as a school librarian and hopes to retire next year. Her son (27) and daughter (30) are both doing well. One of them is working in Miami and the other in San Francisco. Rekha and her husband are still living in the USA.

Maryon Jeane (Howard) I'm still living in a private valley in the middle of Mortimer Forest (bliss!) and still working from home (with my cat, Myrrh, as ever beside me). However the last year or so was rather dramatic and turbulent, as my appendix ruptured spectacularly, resulting in a blue-light dash to Hereford Hospital (which hospital should be avoided at all costs, even if you're in the best of health and strong as an ox). I then discovered at first hand just how poor the state of some hospitals in the NHS has become. Not only did I find it difficult to get out of the wretched place because my blood pressure and temperature measurements (always, throughout my life, on the low side, of which I made the medical staff fully aware from the outset) didn't match their statistics. But I was then scheduled for return because the hospital had managed not only to infect the operation site internally but also had made such a poor job of the thing generally that the entire site ruptured very badly. I dug my heels in and went to a private hospital, Droitwich Spa, for the repair and - oh, the difference to me! I can't say it was an enjoyable experience, but cleanliness, quiet, courtesy, reasonable food, a room of one's own and having people listen properly to information made a whole world of difference as, of course, did proper medical expertise.

However all this meant that I'd lost not only, effectively, over a year out of my normal life, but also most of my clients who, naturally, had to go elsewhere while I was *hors de combat*. This, plus a nearly complete loss of data due to the incompetence of the IT company I employed to sort out my computer (I was unable even to sit at my computer for any period of time, and was definitely unable to get down and dirty with taking it apart), meant a complete rethink as far as work was concerned.

Finally I decided to take a chance and give up having clients and work for myself. So I'm writing a series of practical books, which I'm publishing initially in Kindle format, with associated spin-offs etc. It's great fun and all sorts of things are happening round this venture, such as being sent books and other items free of charge and asked to review them!

I'm enjoying having much more freedom to arrange my days and nights as I wish (I rather like working through the night when it's on my own account) and to sit and think and conjure with ideas. This is what I always wanted and, dare I say it, what education should bring, rather than slavery to a pay cheque and other people's direction.

My partner, Edward, is still doing IT and gains many accolades for troubleshooting difficult projects. He's unfortunately away during most weeks, although sometimes having the chance to work from home, but home at weekends and of course during holidays. (Although he did take the chance of a juice retreat in Portugal when the company offered to pay because he was pretty exhausted, and he had a wonderful time there and came back full of vim and vigour and several pounds lighter.)

We will have been married thirty years this year, which is a ridiculous thought. As I turned sixty in December last year (when it was too cold etc for outside activities), we are celebrating both landmarks by Segwaying and zip-wiring at Leeds Castle for a few days in April (if Miss Venning could take up ballooning in her eighties, I can take up Segwaying and zip-wiring in my sixties!) Onward and upward!

Kok-Tee Khaw Sadly my mother died earlier this year in KL at the age of 89. My husband Pete Taylor retired early last April from his post of Professor in Vascular Surgery in St Thomas's, to spend more time with me he says! Huh! He spends his time doing all the cryptic crosswords! I still work part-time in Tate Millbank. My younger brother Peng-tee was knighted last year, for services to opthalmology in Moorfields and now is Professor Sir! I am very sorry that I'm bragging about him a bit but I am SO pleased about him because he works really hard in both clinical surgery and research.

Claire Linzee (Thomas) was actually in London at the time that I sent out the request for news. She was returning home to Missouri within a few days, and promises to be in touch soon.

Zoe Littleton After many a long year of working for housing associations and as a management consultant, I recently decided to address my work-life balance and start my trial retirement, though I'm still keeping my hand in the affordable housing world as I have just joined the board of a property development company as a non-executive director. I am splitting my time between France (Arles), where my partner is living, and London. Many thanks to the late **Miss Bean** for sparking my love of French/France. In London I now have time, amongst other things, to keep fit and to play tennis again - bringing back distant memories of knock-ups with **Cherry Briggs** (Section 41?), **Tish Golding** and others at Westonbirt.

Sarah Thomas (Leslie) I myself have had rather a bad start to the year. My youngest brother, Simon, died suddenly and unexpectedly at his home in Florida in January. I miss him very much although I did not see him often. He had been going to visit us in August with his 10 year old daughter. We had a lovely thanksgiving service for him at St Mary's in

Richmond, Surrey, and afterwards welcomed guests back at my mother's flat on Richmond Green. It really helped that so many friends and family attended, including **Tish Golding** and other old friends from Kenya days.I have also moved house again.

My sister **Jean Leslie** (Section 41) still lives in Australia but was home for our brother's thanksgiving service. She did not stay long, as she already has a ticket to visit us for three months in May this year, so we are looking forward to seeing her again soon.

Section 42 (1972)
Section representative:
Miranda Purves (Saxby-Soffe)

Jane Barrett Her life improved greatly in August 2013 when she resigned from school. Lovely school, nice children etc but she had become bemired in staffing hassles with someone in her department who was constantly absent, and Jane decided it was time it was somebody else's problem. This worked well until Jane was asked to return and teach an AS pupil some grammar because of problems arising with the same individual. But it is for only three periods a week…

Other highlights have included being part of **Amanda Ross (George)**'s sixtieth birthday celebrations, along with many of her family including her sister Vicky, whom many may remember from the year above us. Jane's own sixtieth birthday was spent in a very windy Alderney, but that is what happens if you are born in February! Jane says that time goes very quickly, and says it is alarming how much better she remembers her time at Westonbirt than so many later events. It seems to have left her with a lifelong dislike of getting up in the morning (that bell!) and she is still amazed at the differing standards of teaching.

Hilary Chester-Master (Fellner) She is still there on the farm, growing and raising local food, selling it through the shop, and cooking it in the café, hosting corporate and training seminars, day and now residential too in their eco conference centre, loving woodland weddings with registrars in wellies, lots of visitors to the yurts, hut, campsite and holiday cottage, hen parties, stags in the woods all keep her out of mischief. She is just starting a project (and hoping Westonbirt might bring a group!) for students from all walks of life (*www.thefarm.education*). If anyone knows a secondary school teacher or youth worker who might be inspired by it, do tell them to get in touch: Hilary would have loved to have done it when she was at school. Luckily both her daughters work with her now and the oldest (of 3) granddaughters already insists on clearing tables in the café at the age of 7, so Hilary hopes to be able to retire soon! She is also in touch with **Nicola Bion** who lives not far away. **Diana Graham (Gantlett)** also visits her when she is in the UK and there is lots to talk about as they are also biodynamic farmers in Oz.

Karen Ciclitira Karen sent in news direct out of the blue, saying that she practises as a psychotherapist in Belsize Park and Harley Street, and also teaches psychology at Middlesex and City Universities. Her daughter Samantha is 11 and is enjoying being at Wellesey House School. Her husband Armand D'Angour teaches classics at Oxford University, and they live in Belsize Park.

Libby Coats (Clover) Libby survived her sixtieth at Christmas, and reminisced about her time in Gloucester Lower Fourth dorm in the autumn of 1966 and its occupants!

Sally Gesua (Clifford) Sally says that her life is pretty good, for which she is thankful. Her daughter has just produced her first grandchild, so that is very special. She sees **Carole Davies (Knight)** sometimes, and is Facebook friends with **Debbie Marr (Cheston)**. Her local sports club has a couple of people from the year above us, and they sometimes talk about olden days at school. One name in particular always seems to crop up! (No prizes for guessing which.) She is still trying to keep fit with lots of running/golf/tennis/swimming, and tries to keep the brain active with competitive bridge (with a forthcoming match against the number one English team!) Unfortunately she suffered hepatitis and a fractured shoulder last year, which put a slight damper on things, but fingers crossed for a healthier year now.

Sally Greensted (Hooker) Sally has not written for a while because she said nothing interesting had happened. However, the past year has had its moments. The day of her reply she had just become a grandmother with her eldest daughter Kate having a daughter of her own who were both fine – just Sally's nerves in shreds. The not so good news was that she was diagnosed with breast cancer last October, since when she has had some fairly unpleasant surgery. Poor **Penny Levinson** happened to call and catch Sally in her hospital bed and was very kind and plied her with magazines and visits.

Rosalie Fowler (Goldingham) Rosalie replied while up to her elbows in marmalade making, with the citrusy smell pervading the house whilst she was waiting for setting point. [Hope it has set by now.] Last year's high spots were a visit on holiday to Vietnam and Cambodia during the spring, followed by daughter Emily's wedding in June. Rosalie is still working four days a week, but feels sure retirement will beckon soon. They keep busy with tennis, table tennis and bridge.

Diana Graham (Gantlett) Diana kindly sent in pictures of Dalmatian turnouts. She lives in the Tropic of Capricorn, 300 km inland from the Queensland coast, so the summer months are hot and humid, and this summer seems to have been all of that. They received plenty of rain, if rather heavy, one storm bringing seven inches of rain in an hour and a half. The country shows all the benefit of the rain and is a sylvan scene at the moment, and the activity of insects is deafening at times, particularly cicadas. The rather murky water in the streams has become clear and sparkling, and so this is a really lovely time if one can ignore the mosquitoes and searing sun. As she wrote, it was too hot and humid for horses to work all day as they develop sores, and so they have been using a helicopter to muster cattle that have to be moved and sorted out. As it brings a lot of cattle together quickly, it puts a lot of pressure on everyone to work quickly so that cattle are not held in yards too long and are quickly moved on to the next fresh area, so it is a mixed blessing as well as fossil-fuel consuming - all to produce organic grass fed beef. The weather should soon move into the less humid cycle, which means that the horses can do this work and this is how they like to run the station.

Diana admits that she no longer goes mustering all day and tends not to ride in the hotter months as she finds herself getting very grumpy after a couple of hours! They are just about to have their wildlife survey, which takes a week, and which she enjoys tremendously as various experts come and look at flora and fauna. The point of it is to look at biodiversity, as well as any impact the cattle have on native species. They have had good results for both flora and fauna so far.

It is particularly interesting to do the night surveys when they look at the arboreal fauna: they have four different gliders (flying possum-like animals) for instance. John and Diana manage to get away for a week or so every six weeks, and usually head to Brisbane or Sydney, often for strategy meetings including the Beyond Fossil Fuel ones. They live in the Gailee Basin which is in the centre of an international effort to prevent the coal being extracted and burnt. They themselves do not have coal underneath them, but it would be absolutely hideous to have this industry polluting their underground water and streams, as well as the destruction of the landscape and even Barrier Reef. One of these mega mines would completely destroy 28,000 ha (75,000 acres), as that would be the size of the open cut mine.

Diana went home in July as her mother was seriously ill, and so spent a couple of months here which she always loves, especially walking and visiting ancient sites and museums/galleries.

She stayed a night with Claud (**Clare Jordan (Gore-Langton)**), who brought her up to date on many things and was on good form. Diana stayed with her sister **Anne** (who was also at Westonbirt, as was her daughter) and one of her brothers.

Diana met **Miranda Bostroem (Cumming-Bruce)** in Brisbane last year as she was over from American for Christmas. They had a fun evening, and Diana met her husband Vanya but missed her children who had returned to England. She also often sees **Hilary Chester-Master (Fellner)**, and keeps in touch with **Deborah Martyr** (who was also in Holford and a year below us), who is still living in Indonesia working for Flora and Fauna International as Chief Campaigner, protecting tigers from poachers, which seems to be an immensely challenging task. She has also published a book on learning Indonesian!

Penny Levinson (Hatchick) Penny was sitting in a hotel in Mumbai at the time of her reply, reading news from almost another world! She too plays bridge (she says very badly) and works at a hospice. As she gets older, she realises how important health is and being able to enjoy every day as you don't know what is around the corner.

Miranda Purves (Saxby-Soffe) I am still involved in local matters, farm, carriage driving and dalmatians. However, I had to have my aged hunter put down last spring, and then Graham (we have been together for 25 years) had to have a heart pacemaker fitted, as he was finding it very difficult to get around. He returned to the farm and seemed to be improving (he was planning business meetings!) when he suffered an immediate and seemingly painless death as I was with him. It was all very traumatic at the time, and the police had to be involved as he was so recently out of hospital. However, his and my families rallied around, and we hopefully gave him the send-off he would have wanted, with four Friesian stallions with all the accoutrements driven by a friend taking him from the farm to the local church in style. Now there is the long business of sorting out all his affairs, with businesses in the UK and the USA. I have recently come to better accept what has happened, and at least I have managed to sell his train set quite quickly which took up room and in which I was not interested!

Guilia Rhodes (Bartrum) Giulia wrote an article in the British Museum Friends' Magazine all about Witches, Demons and Sirens! I am sure her time at Westonbirt had no place in her research.

Joceline San Joceline replied to say that she was still around, despite many years of silence! She is now retired from the rat race, with no regrets. She says life as a pensioner is great and she is enjoying her free travel (thanks to Mayor Boris) and watching all the tennis she wants without guilt. She still exchanges Christmas cards with Keith Riley (Anji's widower), who reminded her that it is now 5 years since Anji died – how time flies. Joceline was also just off to Singapore for a belated Chinese New Year with family. She wished everybody a good Year of the Goat!

Deirdre Waud (Ward) Deirdre says her news is really more of the same. She had managed to prise Chris, her husband, away from his office for long enough to go on a long weekend en famille to Venice for his sixtieth birthday. They also have holidays planned to Egypt, where his godson is getting married, the south of France, and Corsica, to help some friends learn to sail their new catamaran and, hopefully, to the north of Spain for a car rally. Their 'first' over the last year was that it was the first Christmas that both of their girls were gainfully employed (at the ages of 26 and 28!). Deirdre has therefore spent a bit of free cash on upgrading one of their bathrooms and plans to get the outside of the house redecorated (in case one of them gets married at some point!) She is still struggling round the tennis court, playing quite a lot of bridge and spending an increasing amount of time visiting her father who had his 90th last summer.

As a postscript, at the beginning of March there was an obituary in *The Times* for **Charlotte Wynn Parry**'s father who had died aged 90 and for her mother who had died in January.

Since most of our year started at Sedgwick a frightening 50 years ago this year (although there have been some pointed remarks about those who only joined in the Lower Fourth and therefore only 49 years ago), we hope to have a grand reunion this year, and **Sally Gesua (Clifford)** has kindly offered to host us again. Plans are afoot!

Section 41 (1971)
Section representative:
Jennifer Cope

The bad news is that **Jane Eggleston** died last January. Her funeral had a good representation of WBs, and they were **Sally Ann Wilkinson, Gillie Goghlan (West), Celia Jefferies (Thomas), Karen Broomhead (Fielding), Lally St Maur , Sarah Maude, Gill Bray (Ross)** and myself. We will all miss her vitality and friendship. Sadly **Mandy Macdonald** was unable to attend as her mum died that morning.

Tizzie Short (Harbottle) Tizzie is working as a counsellor in London. Her nieces are now at WB.

Nicky Currie (Penley) I took the huge decision to retire from my job as CLA regional director at Christmas to restore my work-life balance. I now have a part-time role promoting the apprenticeship system to employers in the food and farming sector in Suffolk. It's perfect and four-day weekends are great. My father celebrated his 99th birthday just after Christmas, thoroughly enjoying having all his family there, but very sadly he died a month later, and I am on my way to deal with all that goes with the end of an era as I write. I have been very lucky to have his advice and support for so long, but no matter how much one knows no-one can live for ever, it is still a huge blow when it comes. On the plus side, our daughter Alex is getting married in May, which is very exciting, and later that month I have been invited to the garden party at Buckingham Palace as recognition of all I did at the CLA, the Country Land and Business Association.

Section 40 (1970)

Section representative:
Jennifer Cope

Barbie Matthews (Powell) We have had a really good year and feel very fortunate. Peter retired last May, and we found lots of reasons to holiday last year. We celebrated our 40th wedding anniversary and had a lovely summer celebration party.

We bought a caravan. It was a very quick decision, and we have had some lovely few days away during the winter and will enjoy this summer. We have several long weekends planned around England. The next one is to start another long-distance walk with friends, and we are going to Bath for three nights. It is certainly a lovely way to explore and is very luxurious, excellent shower and all cooking facilities including a microwave!

I seem to keep very busy, enjoying helping with the three grandchildren in Buckinghamshire, bridge, quilting and still running my card business.

June Barrow-Green I'm still working at the Open University, doing research in the history of mathematics. Last year, with the anniversary of the start of the First World War, my work on British mathematicians during the War (ballisticians, aerodynamicists and pacifists) got quite an airing, and I have given quite a few talks in schools on the history of women in mathematics. Also, to my complete astonishment, I won an international prize for my academic writing. It's the first time I have ever won anything like that, which just shows it is never too late! Travel for work included South Korea for the first time, while travel for play included a week of triathlon training in the Dordogne, and a 25K race around Spetses in very warm sun. We had a lovely Christmas with sister **Belinda** and family in Somerset, although we all missed my mother and Pightley.

I see a lot of **Lee Twist (Beanland)** and her family as her children are all living round the corner from me in Islington, and also **Shan Rigby (Jones)** who is very active in the Green Party and standing in the forthcoming general election. Very conveniently, Shan and Bill moved to Knaresborough just in time for the Tour de France, and I had a wonderful weekend with them whizzing on a bike around the beautiful Yorkshire countryside following the Tour! I also regularly chew the cud with **Clare Jordan (Gore Langton)** - she is always a good fund of WB gossip!

Clare Keep (Morton) I've been helping a friend with a mare and foal plus companion pony for the last 8 months. In between times, I act as a gopher with her when we take her daughter's horse to dressage events around the area. Recently found myself at a venue in Cirencester across the way from where I once won a set of knives at a fair while at WB! I have also been helping the in-laws to downsize to care accommodation. Our family keeps us entertained with their pursuits, son with his photos of his new property and sporting events in Australia, even one of their PM on his racing bicycle. I still ride and swim, and once the weather warms up, I hope to get back on the bicycle.

Section 39 (1969)
Representative:
Liz Jubb (Grant)

Louise Dixon I sort of come and go. I'll be in the UK in April for two weeks and no doubt in the autumn, but no fixed dates. We are both retired, but I'm on the board of the AA in South Africa and that brings me here four times a year. Suits me well, as I love the country. Euan only comes over once a year.

Ann Foxon Foxy mentions her fitness regime, and I can vouch for the results: she looked stunning when we had a section reunion lunch last year! She writes: "I am now living in Kent. Whitstable was an ideal choice being about an hour from London and lots of things to do around here if you are single, which I still am. It is also good inspiration for artists, which I still am. I bike and walk a lot, exercising two Jack Russells, and when I have time I am researching early British history. Sound like a "bluestocking"? There's nothing wrong with that so long as you wear them in a cool, funky way!"

Noni Graham (Paton) Not a huge amount of news. We have finally finished educating the two boys who now have two degrees apiece and are both self-sufficient right now. Long may it last! However, I have no intention of retiring, and we are looking forward to welcoming B&B guests here and in The Garden Studio as usual. We also continue to run our property rental business. We enjoyed a marvellous holiday on the island of Harris last summer and have booked a ten-day trip in the Outer Hebrides in June to explore some more. We have one son in London and one in Madrid, and so that provides more opportunity for travel.

Caroline Heaton-Watson (McKane) Last year was busy but great fun. The main event was the wedding of our younger daughter Fenella to a fellow schoolteacher. It was a beautiful sunny summer day in Evian les Bains on the shores of Lake Geneva, a stunning location close to where we live part of the year. She and Tony then moved immediately to Zug in Switzerland, where they both teach in an international school. Lucy and Alex and toddler Arthur live at the other end of Switzerland near Geneva. Our son Dom continues to work at Knight Frank and enjoys the lifestyle in Kuala Lumpur. So we usually have a trip planned to visit somebody!

Over the year Richard and I project managed the entire rebuild of our house and garden in Battersea with only the front wall remaining. It's been quite stressful at times, but we are still on speaking terms with our builders after fifteen months. Nearly at an end, and we are really pleased with how it has turned out. Now we are looking forward to enjoying it!

Liz Jubb (Grant) Another year has flown by, mainly because we have had so many visitors, which is lovely but exhausting! We are both heavily involved in local activities (why is there always such a shortage of volunteers?!) which does mean we have got to know an enormous number of people. I am now a fully-fledged guide for Sherborne Abbey, a wonderful building which I never tire of visiting. Music, photography, gardening and walking continue to give enormous pleasure, and Phil and I have carried on with our weekly Away Days which has seen us visit most parts of Dorset and the neighbouring counties. We had a wonderful holiday in Bude last summer where we met up with **Clare Monro (Rust)** and hopefully we will see each other again this year with **Jo Leadbetter (Salz)**. Otherwise, it's much the same as last year: a hugely enjoyable existence!

Jo Leadbetter (Salz) Really enjoying living in Cornwall most of the week, so close to the sea. After a couple of sessions paddle boarding, I now have my own board. More relaxing than surfing! Tarquin's Gin and Cornish Pastis are selling well and now being drunk in Italy, Denmark and Australia. The whole family has become involved in various ways, apart from elder son Duncan who is working hard as a trainee eye surgeon in Exeter, visiting quite often with the lure of the surf. My daughter Athene and I are just back from an epic ten-day trip driving around our island. The country looking quite relaxed pre-election!

Denette Matthews (Skeil) The last year has whizzed by with a lot of sailing through the summer and then shooting taking over from mid-September onwards. Always a gregarious group of friends around for both activities,so good fun. I did manage to catch up with **Jane Williams** when we were in Ireland for Cork Week and had a lovely day out with her and Johnnie. Unfortunately, I have not been in touch with anyone else. All those good intentions came to nothing!

Kate McDowall replied to say she has no news this year.

Lindsay Moffat (Thomas) Getting through the winter here can be quite a job sometimes, especially when I spend so much time outside. We had a truly magical wedding here last May when my son was married with marquee, band and disco. To everyone's great surprise, my elder daughter made her debut in the band as well. The celebrations went on for three days, and it was fantastic to have so many family members and friends to join in. After that, three beautiful foals arrived who kept me busy all summer. As anyone who has experience with horses knows, it is never plain sailing, and there were quite a few problems to deal with amongst the rest of the herd along with everything else, but the foals are fine! Now we are waiting for the arrival of my first grandchild in June. As things get closer, one's apprehension rises so fingers crossed.

Clare Monro (Rust) Hugh and I much enjoyed celebrating our Ruby Wedding by spending a month in the States visiting old friends and old haunts! In 1977/78, after a year working out there we drove 10,000 miles round the US, and back across Canada, in six weeks. This time we 'flew' round, literally, in four, and it was magic. Highlights were lots of visits to the Smithsonian and a wonderful exhibition by artist Andrew Wyeth in Washington. We swam in the Boiling River, Yellowstone National Park, where it met the cold Gardiner River, explored Monhegan Island, Maine, close to Andrew Wyeth's Island, after which we were taken to a wonderful exhibition by son Jamie Wyeth in Rockport, Maine. We now enjoy the fact that our young grandson is living in Kent rather than

Singapore after they moved back to London in February. Although it's a fair old trek from Cornwall, it's certainly closer than the Far East!

Caroline Monty (Tanner) I was glad to go to the Westonbirt carol concert in Fulham, and to meet **Jackie Woodgate (Olsen)**. We had a good natter. I do hope more people come next year.

My sons are both living nearby now, one just gone to Tulse Hill, south of Brixton which is so smart these days, brought about by the advent of the Victoria Line. He works in the computer games industry. Number two son lives in Clapham and is studying law at BPP. It's nice to have lunches and catch up, and offer support still where needed (food usually!) I'm still battling with my sibling committee disputes and my mother, which is a nightmare. I suspect I am not alone in this. My partner, Chris, is very supportive.

I did enjoy a trip alone to Greece in September. I just took off like I used to in my twenties. It was heaven. There's a whole swathe of people who island-hop all summer, and good company was readily available when wanted.

Daphne Oliver-Bellasis (Parsons) We are very well and seem to be as busy as ever. We went out to visit Joanna and Andrew in Whistler, Canada last September. It was lovely to see the village in the summer, having only seen it covered in snow before. Nicola and Tom are now back in England as Tom has left the Army. They have just had a little daughter, Amelia, who is very sweet.

Fleur Potamianos (Kitchen) The plug-hole is ever nearer: no one knows what to do and it's a little nervewracking. The weather is vile here at the moment, but spring is creeping in - lots of daffs out and blossom. I'm no longer active career-wise, but very active as a child carer (the grandchildren) and with various organisations helping the very many needs of the poor here, also with the Red Cross. We have more than 1.5 million migrants in Greece, all in camps or hiding out with no papers and desperate. They are all trying to get through Greece and on to the UK, but the borders here on the west coast are controlled by the EU, so they can't move on. The EU Directive is to send them home, but they rarely want to do that.

Jill Powell (Fawkes) It will be good to get the WB news via online in future. We were skiing in Lake Louise for a week, then I went a bit further west into the Bugaboo mountains for a second week (heli-skiing with friends). All great fun and plenty of snow. Now it looks like spring is well on the way, lots of bulbs coming up and I hope to get busy in the garden before long.

Angie Rose (Waite) Thankfully my life continues as normal - and continues! So nothing noteworthy to report but glad to hear from you.

Lizzie Speller (Moore) My last year has been a busy one, mostly because my latest book was set in WWI. I've done a round of centenary-connected events, from tiny bookshops and reading groups to literary festivals and huge auditoriums, and from London to Edinburgh, to cities and towns all over England, as well as Brussels and France, where my St Malo hotel was right on an endless and beautiful beach outside the old town ramparts. I was on a very amusing, interesting and loud panel on war fiction with Alan Hollinghurst and William Dalrymple. Now I am about to fly off to Syracuse in the US where the snow is thick, apparently, as my latest book, *At Break of Day,* (called *The First of July* there) is Central New York State's One Read. After that, one last talk in Salisbury in May and then I settle down, not just to my new book, but rather neglected children and grand-daughters!

Sally-Anne Thomas I've had a busy year, still on a slight high after my escape from BBC News. There was another trip to Australia, for my great-nephew's wedding in Canberra and a whistle-stop tour of relatives. On the way, I stopped in Tokyo. I've never been to Japan before. What an interesting place! Going to Australia in winter is not to be recommended. Everyone at home assumes you're sunning yourself on a beach, but in fact it was freezing, and when I went with my nieces to a Brumbies' match (Rugby Union, for the uninitiated), we huddled up under a blanket and drank alternate swigs of hot coffee and wine.

I came back in time to fulfil my volunteer role at the Commonwealth Games in Glasgow. I was on the Protocol team, looking after the 'Games family' - officials and VIPs. Apart from not recognising Prince Edward, I did pretty well. Danny Alexander ate sandwiches moodily in our lounge, Alex Salmond lorded it like the Young Pretender (this was before the referendum.) A pleasant woman hugged me and thanked me for all I was doing. It was only when she left and I said "What a nice lady" that I discovered it was Dame Kelly Holmes. I'm not very good on athletes. Ended up the week protecting Usain Bolt from journalists after he'd made his ill-advised remark about the Commonwealth Games being "rather sh*t". It felt weird to be on the other side of the fence! I stayed in our French house for two months, gradually slowing down and policing the dogs as they menaced locals and tourists. Aggie caught a mouse and Lulu dug up a dead mole.

This year I've been to Athens, meaning to have an orgy of museum visiting. It snowed! I stayed in a wonderful hotel overlooking the Acropolis and the Temple of Athenian Zeus, and was very tempted to stay in the warm and just drink in the view.

Earlier this month was Crufts, and Agrippina Julia Augusta and I were on duty on the Cirneco dell'Etna stand for four days, answering the same questions: "I've never seen one before, how many of them are there?", "How do you pronounce that?", "Are they Pharaohs?" I've been doing my usual freelance writing, fact and fiction, and in May I shall be working as a BBC stringer at the general election count for Harrow East and West.

Shelagh Tonkyn (McNeice) I don't really have anything new to add in the way of news. Still doing my work in the courts, increasingly on the Family Panel rather than the adult criminal court since, sadly, family work seems to be the growth area. There are major changes taking place, which will hopefully result in a better service for children and families and reduce the delays which are so damaging to children's lives.

Health-wise, I'm happy to report that everyone is keeping well and the NHS is doing an excellent job of testing and scanning them all at regular intervals, which is very reassuring. I'm acutely aware of how lucky we are to be benefitting from such care and to be living at a time when cancer research has progressed so much.

Carlo Trotter (Sheppard) I am afraid I have been somewhat out of it. My brother Christopher, who many knew from Westonbirt/Radley high jinks, was in hospital from October and suddenly took a turn for the worse and died in January. He had no current partner or widow, but four children with three different mothers. Also, he had a complicated antique business. I am still busy with the day job and the school governing, as well as organising the funeral and now the memorial service.

Corrie Turner (Leigh) I had a telephone conversation with Corrie who was on excellent form. She is in good health and still training horses. She and I hope to meet up at our local garden centre after Easter.

Jane Williams (Daniell) Great news about the Association News going to be available to order online – will save my problem of not having a sterling account and WB not taking credit cards. I haven't read a booklet for 30 years! The knee replacement operation in February 2014 certainly influenced my activities (or lack of them) for the year. The operation was a success, and now, a year later, I am nearly back to normal, although fitness levels have a way to go. A visit to stay with our daughter and family in early July certainly helped my recovery. I was asked to visit to look after Feargus (18 months) for five days in Bristol while Ciara was busy with the final week teaching and husband Alex was attending a two-day interview. Feargus had just taken delivery of a balance bike (no pedals, two wheels) and was already flying down the pavements in a very alarming way. Nothing for it but to follow at high speed. When I got back to Ireland, Johnny noticed that I had dispensed with my stick and had improved beyond recognition!

We met up with **Denette (Skeil)** during the summer when she visited Ireland for Cork Yacht week. We had a lovely day in Ardmore at the Cliff House Hotel in amazing weather. The views across the bay were stunning and the food was very special too. A memorable meeting where once again we picked up where we left off – we first met in Prep School at Westwing in 1961!

Johnny and I really enjoyed our trip to Venice and Verona in November. We stayed in Riva del Garda in a lovely old hotel. The trip to Venice was far too short, and we promised to return. Verona was very interesting and full of Roman architecture. Johnny continues his treatment and is on a rest period at the moment. He plans to join Ciara, Alex and Feargus and Alex's family near Chamonix at the end of March. It remains to be seen whether the daredevil grandson will take to the skis this year.

We returned to UK at Christmas to stay in Ciara and Alex's new house near High Wycombe. They will be in High Wycombe until next Christmas, when they make the big move to somewhere in the Marlborough area. Alex's interview was successful and he got the much sought after job at Boscombe Down in Crash Analysis.

Our son Justin and partner Emer are holidaying in Mexico. It is incredible that we get non-stop pics via WhatsApp so quickly. It looks wonderfully warm and relaxing. Justin is delighted with his new job in Investec, having left Allied Irish Bank after nearly ten years. Emer is a solicitor working in the Central Bank.

My Mum celebrates her 90th birthday next week. I will make a day trip to meet my brother in Bristol and travel down to Burnham-on-Sea to see her and go out for lunch. She is in good form and doesn't miss much, but finds the great-grandchildren's noise levels a bit challenging!

Between the GIY (grow it yourself) group, doing registrations for the Welsh Pony Association, and part-time work at Goresbridge Sales, I seem to keep fairly busy. Our Welsh Section A pony is leased this year, and I am looking forward to seeing him compete in showjumping and working hunter with his eight year old rider Sallyanne. That's about it for this year. Best wishes to the rest of Section 39.

Jackie Woodgate (Olsen) I went to the Carol Concert at Christmas with Karen which was really lovely. I thought the singing was just gorgeous - takes me back. I also met **Carolyn (Tanner)**. We sat together and just chatted and chatted as if we were old friends despite the fact that I had already left WB by the time Carolyn arrived.

We have not sold our house as yet and have currently taken it off the market, as people have seemingly lost the desire to live in the country. It appears that everyone now wants to live in Clifton Village with its gorgeous boutiques and coffee shops.

But things will change fairly quickly when the ridiculous parking restrictions instigated by the Mayor of Bristol George Ferguson come into force at the end of March. People won't think Clifton living is so great then!

Since last writing we are very excited that our younger daughter Louisa is soon to be a mummy. She is due in about 5-6 weeks so things are really speeding up. As we are first time grandparents. we are so excited/nervous and wondering what is going to hit us! She and her partner John decided to find out in advance whether it is a boy or girl, and to our delight it is a little boy. They currently live in West London at the end of Kensington High Street near Olympia in a lovely spacious flat, but I would hazard a guess that they will want somewhere with a garden fairly soon. They also have a gorgeous little cocker spaniel, so a garden is high on their agenda. I have been invited to come for the first couple of weeks when the little chap arrives, so I had better brush up on my baby skills - I feel somewhat panic stricken at the moment!

Angi Young (Fowler) Angi has had a miserable year with serious health issues. I am in touch with her and she remains cheerful and works part-time to take her mind of things. I am sure we all wish her well.

Section 38 (1968)
Representative:
Chris Shaw (Morris)

Alison Andrews (Maggie Morgan) Both my parents died in the past two years, both having reached 99 and being more than ready to go. I'm finally allowed to be a grown-up, and am finding retirement the best career ever. Reading masses, knitting obsessively, supporting stressed daughters with their children, and still trying to persuade thinking people to vote Lib Dem. Or, in the case of the Independence Referendum, to vote No Thanks. Such a relief that I don't have to carry through the threat of moving to France! Instead I'm trying to buy a plot of land with planning permission, right beside the beach near my grandmother's cottage in Argyll. I've inherited a quarter share of the original cottage but the ideal is to have a house of my own. If it works, I will be issuing invitations in about four years' time. Visitors should bear in mind what local MP Danny Alexander says: "There's no such thing as bad weather in Lochaber. Just inappropriate weather."

Sue Bottell (Rigley) wrote that she was not sending any news this year as it was very much the same as last year's news, but she gets a couple of honourable mentions in Alison's report below!

Julia Douglas (Neath) came to stay with me in Tetbury early last summer, and we very much enjoyed taking part in the visit to the gardens at Highgrove organised through the Westonbirt Association. Julia writes:

This has been the year of The Move for the Douglases. Having decided to make a move back to Sevenoaks where we had lived seven years previously, we found a house in a very central location in the town which was in severe need of renovation. This proved to be irresistible to John who always delights in a project. Although work began last June, it has only been habitable since December, and although virtually 90% complete, there are still a few things which remain outstanding. Overall, though, we are very satisfied with the final outcome and greatly enjoy the convenience of being able to walk both to the station and to the centre of the town in less than 10 minutes.

Unfortunately the move has taken us a little further away from Oxted, where eldest daughter Laura and family live with their two children, but it is still a manageable journey, and we have a regular babysitting slot over there every Friday afternoon.

Our other grandchild Fred is much further away, however, in Rio de Janeiro to be precise, where son Bruce is working as a freelance reporter. Younger daughter Mia is living and working in London, which is more readily accessible than Brazil from our point of view! For obvious reasons we have not done any long distance travelling this year (having made two visits to Brazil at the start of last year), but hope to rectify that once we retrench financially after all the final expenses on the new house have been paid out.

We had a truly delightful weekend down in Christchurch, Dorset this time last year attending the wedding of Chris Shaw's son Andrew – the sun shone relentlessly and we enjoyed every moment of our visit. I also see **Judy Kramer (Nettleton)** from time to time, whenever she comes over to the UK to visit her now elderly mum in Littlehampton, and we usually chew the cud over a very tasty fish-and-chip lunch along the promenade!

Diana Gale (Forwood) I am less stressed this year with both boys happily at university, my father's flat let out, and me fully retired. I play tennis regularly and do good deeds such as helping out at a community market and Fairtrade stall. I'm going to German classes, revision mostly, but there are lots of topics we didn't cover in 1968, such as healthy living, recycling and renewable energy. I went to Stuttgart last October when John had a business trip there, and I'm hoping to go with him to

Augsburg this coming October, so plenty of opportunities to practise. The other highlight of the year was doing a two-day cricket scorers' course, with an exam at the end (that people fail!) but I was amazed to get a certificate with 93% on it. So you now know what I'll be doing this summer. Let's hope for warm, sunny weekends.

On Sunday I am going to **Annabel Kerr (Johnston)**'s new grandson Theo's christening. I had a Christmas letter from **Hilary Hughes (Moore)** who is still in Brisbane, but not retiring yet as she enjoys her University library work. Hilary also has a young grandson.

Alison Gauld (Taylor) I must apologise for not having replied last year. So I really need to give you two years' news. We enjoyed Sam Bottell's wedding in Northern Ireland and a tremendous trip to the States where we met up with Peter and **Penny Bysshe (Osborn)** and cruised back on the Queen Mary II together. We visited my Dutch pen-friend, introduced through the Guides at WB, for her 65th birthday at Easter. At Whitsun we flew to Spain to stay with my godson and new wife at their villa near Murcia. Then to celebrate our silver wedding anniversary, we had a wonderful trip to Florence and Siena with a private guide and limo for the whole week. We visited Paul and **Sue Bottell (Rigley)** in the Isle of Man, and it is always good to see them.

Jim changed his job and now works for Sopra Steria as Director of Business Transformation. My mother (91) has been in a nursing home for the last two years, and sadly she now has moderate dementia. My father (92) lives at home still, with a live-in carer. My sons and their families are all fine, and I have four delightful grandchildren, so I spend a lot of time visiting them all.

Hobbies still include bridge (where I became a National Master at 60), Pilates, organising an outings group for the elderly, and being a volunteer hospital driver and coordinator. Since developing Sjogren's Syndrome, I am adapting to modern technology and thoroughly enjoying audible books on my i-phone. Sadly I have had to give up sewing and Deadly Killer Sudokus because of the dry eyes. I am very involved with my local church as a sacristan, server and administrant, and am in my eight year as secretary of the finance committee. I am also an area coordinator for the RNLI.

For our joint 65th birthdays Penny and I are going with our husbands to Le Manoir aux Quat'Saisons to celebrate in May.

What a brilliant idea to be able to download the Association News online!

Janet Johnson (Plowright) contacted me to say that nothing much has changed or nothing particularly exciting has happened in her life for the last few years. Of the Oxford contingent she had bumped into **Jane Fisher (Binney)** at both a funeral and a concert, and realised once again that quite a number of their friendship circles are distantly overlapping, but knows woefully little about what Jane is doing herself. Jan said she was very sorry to hear of Miss Bean's death. Me, too! I remember her as an excellent teacher, who always seemed enthusiastic and upbeat. Does anyone else remember the French dining room where those of us studying French spent numerous lunchtimes making stilted and fractured conversation?

Chris Shaw (Morris) For my husband Martin and I, 2014 was an incredibly eventful year which saw so many changes in our lives. We had the proverbial birth, marriage and death in the family - to be exact, my daughter Suzy's son Ralph was born prematurely in November 2013, which meant that I had to rearrange my originally intended January 2014 granny trip to Malaysia (where they live) to go earlier and help out. Luckily Ralph is now a mischievous toddler who shows no signs of having been a premature baby.

My son Andrew was married to Leanne at Easter 2014. The wedding was in a beautiful setting in gardens in front of the ruined Christchurch Priory, with the bonus of warm sunshine. We were delighted that John and **Julia Douglas (Neath)** joined us for the weekend, along with other old friends. Andrew and Leanne are expecting their first baby in May.

In July, my widowed stepmother died peacefully at home aged 93. The intervening months have brought me a load of paperwork, clearing up the estate and trying to sell her flat – never easy when one lives at a distance – as well as the sadness of the end of an era.

After moving out of our own house last spring (a downsizing of sorts), we have been renting in North Yorkshire and are just beginning to househunt in earnest, looking for a smaller house in Harrogate or one of the surrounding villages. At the same time, we have been having alterations done in our Georgian townhouse in Tetbury, which has been tricky to supervise from two hundred miles away. It is listed, so it took us about eighteen months to sort out the plans and the paperwork. However, we are delighted with the finished result and hope to spend more time there now that Martin has finally retired from the law. He finished at the end of October, and we both enjoyed all the farewell jollies.

However, everything was put on hold in the last couple of months of the year. As the result of a prostate biopsy (thankfully clear) he developed sudden sepsis and was rushed to hospital with a life-threatening infection. The irony of having nothing actually wrong, but developing such a severe infection from the test!

We had to cancel our post-retirement holiday visit to Malaysia and Singapore while he convalesced. Luckily he is now fully recovered, and we can finally embark on retirement.

I made a flying visit on my own to see Suzy, Luke and Ralph at Marlborough College. Malaysia in January, belatedly delivering their Christmas presents. I am hoping that 2015 will be an easier year for us all.

Diana Sichel (Ferguson) says her daughter Buzz is to be married in July to a doctor. His name is Dr Toby Dean, and his brother's girlfriend Nicola is **Jane Weston's** daughter. John and Dee see Simon and **Jane Fisher** as they are all based in Oxford. Jane and Simon always send a comprehensive summary of their year in their Christmas card. They are both still doing a lot of counselling and humanitarian work, both at home, in Africa and elsewhere in the world.

Lovely, as ever, to hear what you are all up to. Keep well and busy ... and, of course, in touch!

Section 37 (1967)
Section Representative:
Jenifer Davidson (Moir)

Sultana Al-Quaiti (Rashid) Sooty is very much looking forward to hosting her section at home in East Sheen for a lunchtime get-together on May 10th and a wander round Richmond Park where she grew up. Muzna is expecting a baby around that time which will bring the number of grandchildren to six. Saleh and Fatima are well in Abu Dhabi. Her osteoarthritis is troubling her more and more as she gets older.

Alison Boxley (Muir) NZ is great. I love it here and really feel at home. Have made lots of new friends and am involved in all sorts of local activities from packing flour at the local co-operative whole food shop to quilting and knitting with various groups. I also walk every morning with a group of women at 7.30am, ending at a coffee shop of course! And there are evenings of gardening at each others' houses and other evenings drinking wine.

Have recently done the four-day Queen Charlotte walking track with two friends from Britain and am looking forward to some good walking this summer in Britain and Ireland.

Last September five of us (including **Cas Botham-Whetham**) did half of Offa's Dyke walk from north to south. We had brilliant weather and lots of fun.

Jenifer Davidson (Moir) Managed to fall down stairs and break my wrist in the summer, just as I was due to go south for a family wedding. Did make my niece's wedding in September up at Aboyne. Apart from that still busy working, playing tennis and doing aquafit. Good to see some Westonbirt girls in the Welsh team for the U19 Home International Lacrosse tournament, which is in Edinburgh. Also looking forward to the U19 World Championships here later in the year.

Section 36 (1966)
Representative:
Julia Braggins (Cock)

Moi Beveridge (Adamson) I am still stag-hunting, in a desultory fashion, mostly in the car. I am praying for a workable Tory majority so might get a repeal of Cherie's social hang-up. I went to the reunion last October which was disappointing, with no-one in our section there, and rather made to feel like second class citizens. Lunch in servants' dining room by Hades and had to be escorted over the school by pupils. Shall give it one more shot to see if any better. Of course next year (2016) is the 50th anniversary of our section leaving so might be a better turn-out.

I am still battling with the horrors of a computer. Don't laugh, but I had to buy a 'new' IBM typewriter online as the 1976 model died at a crucial moment.

Red deer come up to my French windows to be fed, literally feet away (don't seem to mind unsexy winceyette nightie), and I don't tell them that I hunt them as well.

Julia Braggins (Cock) We were thrilled to welcome a new grandson, Harry, born on April 23rd (Shakespeare's birthday and St George's Day: 'Cry God for Harry, England and St George'!) He was the first baby for our youngest daughter Emily. Having had three girls ourselves, we now have one grand-daughter and four grand-sons, aged from seven downwards, so we are getting used to childcare at rather a different tempo.

In September 2014 I had a new knee (old age creeping on apace) and that took quite a bite out of the last part of the year. It takes a while to get back to full steam. Peter was a brilliant nurse and housekeeper. He has finally stepped back from his role supporting young teachers on the Teach First programme, and we are both busy doing the sort of family and community things you do at this very rewarding time of life. Big thanks to everyone who wrote in. I love to hear everyone's news.

Judy Chesterman (Clarke) This has been a year of upheaval for the Chesterman family. We came home from a lovely holiday in Tuscany in May to a daughter who had decided (quite rightly) that it was time to fly the parental nest. After much discussion, we decided that the obvious answer was to sell our family home of 31 years and downsize, thus releasing money to help not only Emma, but Mark and his family as well. So that's what we did, and in October we moved into a smaller, 1960s house round the corner. It needed a huge amount doing to it, so we have been living with the builders for some time. At the end of this month (February), they have to down tools for an indefinite period, as Mark, Katrina and Sophia (2) are moving in. They've sold their house, but their purchase fell through, and they have had to start again, so they could be here for some months. Meanwhile, we have found a great little house for Emma, but it is also full of builders! They are under pressure now to finish next week so that she can move her mass of stuff out of our house before her brother's family move theirs in. Just as well loads of ours is in storage. I have continued to work throughout all this, and having to go and stay in a hotel in Stratford from time to time has become a haven of peace!

Sarah Ferguson Last May I was delighted to hold another reunion at Knoll House Hotel, with walks in the dunes, on the beach and downland. We made good use of our free passes by taking the bus to visit the Russell Coates Museum in Bournemouth. Eyes closed, we could have been taken for a group of schoolgirls, giggling and chattering on a day out.

In June I went to Morocco for a yoga retreat and worked the summer season gardening and flower arranging at the hotel. As I write this, I am in Northland, New Zealand, continuing to enjoy their summer, having spent more time in the South Island on this visit. I'll be back in the UK for Easter and the summer season.

Lucy Fisher (Sadleir) My son Tim and his girlfriend had a beautiful baby boy last June, Laurie Blake Fisher, so I am a very happy granny with a granddaughter and grandson. Ian and I have known each other nearly 10 years now, and he has recovered well from the stroke he suffered 18 months ago. We had a lovely holiday in Menorca last June and have just booked to return this year. I play a certain amount of bridge, enjoy weekly yoga and monthly NADFAS meetings and occasional trips with them, including *Top Hat* this Wednesday in Birmingham.

Sandy Marshall (Hellawell) I am now into my third year of retirement, though still doing some freelance work in educational publishing. This led to another working visit to Trinidad at the end of January. I hadn't expected another at this age! Singing in a choir continues to lead to interesting places. We sang in Odessa in February 2014, even as protests were gathering pace in Kiev. An opportunity arose which seemed unusual: to sing Verdi's *Requiem* in Mumbai in February this year and to extend the trip to see some famous sights - interesting if exhausting.

Karen Olsen Several members of my year, split between sections 36 and 37, once again met at **Sarah Ferguson**'s family hotel in Dorset early in May 2014. We had a great few days catching up, and most of the time the weather held. **Christine Dayananda (Dias)** joined us from Sri Lanka, so it was good to see her, as the last time we met up was in Newport when she was over with her husband in 2010. Thanks go to Sarah for organising such an enjoyable break.

Sultana Al-Quaiti (Rashid) is hosting this year's reunion (2015) at her house in south-west London. Hopefully a few more of us can get to hers for Sunday 10 May. The Association had a most enjoyable trip to Highgrove last year. Only 26 could go as that is the maximum number allowed for a booking. However, those on the waiting list will get first refusal this year, as we are booking a further trip.

I so enjoyed the School Carol Service at Parsons Green, in London, in December. Thanks to the school for arranging the event. The school Chamber Choir came up and helped swell the singing. They also did a beautiful anthem based on the hymn "In the Bleak Mid-Winter" and a flute trio played "Ding Dong Merrily". I brought my sister **Jackie Woodgate (Olsen)**, and she enjoyed meeting up with a new member from her year, **Carolyn Monty (Tanner),** now in Section 39. It was good to catch up with **Eileen McGregor (Bond)** who read one of the lessons, and many others who were there as well. Hopefully we will do a repeat in London again this year.

Alison Palmer (Wheeler) The grandchildren grow, now the boys are 10, 8 and nearly 7, and Rosa is nearly 8. My job working for our local MP Sir George Young is coming to an end as he is standing down at the next election in May, and I am redundant. Not sure what I shall do, but I think something. We still do BandB, which has been very busy this year. My Mum (93) has recently had a fall, so we have a carer looking after her until she is better.

We have a wonderful trip planned to Gallipoli and Istanbul this autumn with all my husband's family. We are going because his grandfather was killed at Gallipoli, and it is the 100th anniversary. We have a Turkish friend organising the trip, and he has found us a wonderful guide to take us to all the places we want to visit.

Alison Parry (Sturdy Morton) I survived a life-defining year, moving house, getting divorced and a spell in emergency care in New Orleans. I had to move in five weeks from the large family home of thirty years and was then homeless for a few months. I am now trying to squeeze into a small one-bedroom flat in the Barbican. Actually, I love my new flat in its concrete jungle, and the central location means I can visit theatres more regularly and almost on a sudden whim! My divorce was finalised in December, so I am now free to make my own decisions about life and plan more travelling. I have spent several months this year in Guadeloupe enjoying life with my four-year-old granddaughter. New Year celebrations on the beach were especially memorable, with dancing in the sand and a midnight swim with fireworks in the distance. For any *Death in Paradise* fans, it is filmed in Guadeloupe, and we visited some of the locations and got caught up in the filming, though not on film!

I finally visited Petra, which was as amazing as I had always imagined. In fact the first sighting of the famous treasury building was better than all expectations and Petra by night quite romantic. One should, however, definitely see it in daylight first for that initial heart-stopping moment. Jordan was a revelation, with excellent Roman ruins, and beautiful countryside, and quite extraordinarily almost everyone spoke perfectly accented English.

A road trip in September through Alabama to New Orleans was great fun. However, a bad, immediate and almost fatal case of shellfish poisoning meant I ended up in hospital, through the fortunate quick thinking of someone calling an ambulance, and the paramedics keeping me breathing. I do not remember anything from shortly after leaving the restaurant until many hours later when leaving the hospital and being returned to my hotel bed, but I am very glad to have survived to tell the tale!

Our May reunion in Dorset was totally fantastic, thank you so much, Sarah. It was great fun to spend a few days exploring the ancient countryside, chatting and eating. Amazing how young we have all remained!

Griselda Pollock When **Julia Braggins** phoned Griselda, she was "stunned"! WB wasn't heaven for her as she felt like a misfit. It may have been tainted by the fact that her mother died in 1964, hence she never made the sixth form. She is now a professor of C19th Art History at Leeds University, has written nine reference books, has a son and daughter and a husband, also a professor at Leeds. I gave her all the news and said I would keep in touch.

Tilly Roberts De Zagal (Roberts) It's been a very busy and happy year. I sold my home in Santiago of 36 years. It took me approximately nine months to sort through so much stuff. I managed to have it all (what was left of it) shipped to the garage of my weekend cottage where I now live.

I've bought a flat in Santiago which will be ready in June. I've never lived in a flat before and am loving living in the countryside.

Diane Stibbard (Brocklehurst) Our eldest daughter got married last August, a lovely day that they organised mostly themselves. Robin and Helena make a handsome couple. We as usual took off for New Zealand after Christmas, via Doha and Bali and back via Australia. Harriet, our other daughter, has her own flat and is in banking. Loving her independence! We still live in Wiltshire and are considering turning the basement in London into a flat for future years. With other building works also on the horizon, spending hours learning and playing bridge, and a visit to Florence in May, 2015 looks like a busy year.

Section 35 (1965)
Section Representative:
Marilyn Jones (Bird)

Philippa Dutton (Thomson) At last I retired from my job as Assistant Secretary of the Royal Warrant Holders Association at the end of June, after 17 happy years. The members were very generous, and the sum they collected enabled me to buy a decent replacement violin and bow, my good instrument having been stolen in 1997. I also attended various parties in my honour, and was touched by the fuss made of me by everyone and the generosity of their gifts. I was awarded an MVO in The Queen's Birthday Honours and my investiture by Her Majesty The Queen on 11 November was a truly memorable day.

After 6 months at home I have taken a short-term contract in the Royal Garden Party office at Buckingham Palace, which I am much enjoying. With security clearance for 10 years, there may be other opportunities for short-term employment in the future.

Meanwhile my husband Dickie and I are taking every advantage of at last having more time together. We had another visit to India in January, and there are plans afoot for travel in Europe from June onwards, as well as a return trip to Turkey in September. Both of us enjoy singing in our various choirs and I have adjusted to a life away from full time office work very quickly.

After 50 years since we left school, I was thrilled to meet up with **Caroline Revitt**, **Lindy Bawtree** and **Janet Welsford** last summer. It was such fun catching up with news and I hope to see them regularly in the years to come.

Marilyn Jones (Bird) I keep busy with much travelling (Bhutan, Malaysia, Thailand, India, Greece, Tobago, and a 40-day cruise to

Singapore in Jan/Feb), and spending time with our seven grandchildren, four of whom live in Malaysia – hence a good excuse to travel!

Sian King (Davies) I have recently enrolled at our local university to do a PhD in 17th century book history (never too late!) I have also acquired, rather unexpectedly, a part-time job as an administrator at Newport Cathedral, which is continuing to provide an interesting insight into the running of a cathedral, especially learning about the Church in Wales, which is different, in many ways, from the Church of England.

Our house building project is progressing well (four years on!), and we have reached the internal painting stage. By this time next year, there's a chance we shall have moved in. I have also taken up a voluntary post as governor at the local large further education college, am secretary of the Friends of the Newport Ship and do a bit of transcribing for Gwent Archives.

Section 34 (1964)
Representative:
Julia Popham (Bishop)

Ann Beattie (Buckland) Not much news to report. John and I have visited various places in the UK this last year. Nothing very adventurous as John's back doesn't allow for too much long distance travelling by car. However, we hope to visit friends in Saumur in late summer as we can fly from London City, which is very convenient from Canterbury. I'm glad that the News is going online. I'm sure that will be good for a lot of people.

Clare Carter (Binney The first half of the year I kept busy with my U3A activities, including a visit to Spain to see Seville, Cordoba and Granada, which I'd always wanted to see. I also had a quick but hectic trip to Brittany with the choir that I sing with. Spent part of July in England, family wedding and seeing friends, including a day at Hampton Court Flower Show.

The rest of the year has been a bit different, as, after felling unwell for a while, I've been diagnosed with lymphoma, for which I'm now having chemotherapy. This has a good success rate, and so far has not been too trying, so I'm just looking forward to picking up everything again later in the year. Both the children have been over, and it's been lovely seeing them. I had to cancel a trip to Japan in the autumn when they would both have been there which was very disappointing. Hope to have more interesting news next year!

Mary Cave (Rawlence) I heard from **Elizabeth Ells (Rawlence),** who is Mary's sister and lives in Canada. Elizabeth writes as follows: "My sister Mary remains amazingly cheerful, despite the increasing disabilities imposed by multiple sclerosis. Her husband, Christopher, is a stalwart partner and her daughter also lives close by." (Mary and her husband live in Croydon.)

June Cohen (Kefford) Not quite such an exciting year, personally, as last year, but nonetheless a good one for us all. Husband, Clive, has been 'de-retired' for the last nine months which has meant a heavy workload for him and some re-adjustment for us both. However, happily re-retirement is only a month away! I continue to enjoy tennis, gardening, singing, school governing and furthering my family history research and writing. A few church commitments keep me out of mischief, but I have swapped the arduous national selection advising for a much less pressured diocesan pre-selection role.

On the family front we have added little Zoe, born in November, to our small clutch of grandchildren, Ed and Helen's first baby. All five are such a joy, and we are so very lucky that they and our children are all in this country, and we manage to see them often. Our eldest son, Alex, has just been appointed Head of Operations for Bath Rugby Club - overnight he has become by far the most popular member of the family with all the rugby enthusiasts!

Charlotte Essex (Humpidge) Richard celebrated his 70th birthday with a small family party just as he'd been diagnosed with a leaking aortic valve, now being monitored. His year as President of the local Probus Club entailed a lot of extra work alongside our antique fairs. We so enjoyed our holiday in Malta that we returned last year. Unfortunately the weather was disappointing with us experiencing a hurricane! The garden continues to give great joy and produce was good. Grassing over two flower beds has helped to reduce the workload - it's an acre. I'm trying to shed a few voluntary commitments rather unsuccessfully.

I met **Lella Fountaine (Bateman)** at a friend's lunch party - years since we had met, and heard from **Lindy Bawtree**, **Ro Hill (Lloyd Kirk)** and **Sarah Bennison (Nickell-Lean)** at Christmas. Our son, Andrew, continues with his electrical and building business and helps Jo who is running a cafe. It's been a tough year for both of them. Zofia, a very active three year old, often comes to stay at weekends keeping us on our toes. She is a delight. Jonathan is working at Friends Life and went to Thailand again to visit Gail's parents. Catherine is working as a PA for the NHS in a project team aiming to integrate health care, social care and mental health care for people with long term conditions in Southwark and Lambeth - a challenging job which she enjoys.

Susan Fisher (Barritt) David and I returned to the UK last May to start the new adventure of David's retirement. We had four very good years in Dubai, and I did not particularly want to leave. I miss the friends I made and, at this time of year, the sunshine of Dubai. However, I am now happy to be back. and we are settling into our new life in what was our holiday home in Littlehampton over looking the sea.

Anne Grocock Not much news from me this year. I am still busy in Oxford with the NHS and have recently trained as a Mental Health Act manager. In between these activities I still have time to deal with two gardens. I met up with **Chris Bryan** several times. We had a couple of excellent days out last year at Nuffield Place and the Ming Exhibition at the British Museum and recently in Oxford, where we had lunch outside on the roof of the Ashmolean on a very sunny day in February. I did not manage to get to the Association Day at Westonbirt last year, but I am very hopeful that l will be there this year.

Claire Marshall My daughter Emily married Adam Murray, a naval officer, in May last year, under clear open skies - good augury. They now live in rural Nova Scotia, commuting to work in Halifax, east coast snowstorms permitting. Given our own frigid winter (weeks on end of minus 20°C and the canal open to skaters for a record 59 days in a row), it is delightful to think back to my Morocco trip in April last year with all its warmth, colour, spice and unexpected landforms.

This contrasted with Russia in the fall - all golds and fallow fields, endless variations on the onion-dome and art and music galore. I transited directly to Switzerland for a family visit, culminating in six delightful days with **Prue Bishop (Taylor)**, who introduced me to her art and her inspiration in the mountains and gullies of the Haute Savoie.

I've taken on more responsibiliities with the Sistema-inspired music program for inner city kids (OrKidstra) and am thoroughly enjoying the challenge. Still singing - I think I'll be doing that at my own funeral!

Julia Popham (Bishop) Another year has rushed past, and we continue to keep busy with various local activities. We had our son, daughter and two little grandchildren living with us for seven months last year whilst they were doing up their house. We had a few days holiday in Derbyshire in September and have just come back from a short break to Malta with our daughter Clare. We have a couple of trips to France planned for the summer, including a walking holiday. I very much enjoyed seeing **Vicky Schaerer (Lang)** in London when she was over for a short break from Switzerland just before Christmas. It has been lovely to hear from members of my Section, and thanks to all those who contributed news.

Alannah Rylands (Hall) Nothing much happened this year. We are just off to Singapore to see younger daughter and three grandsons from five years downwards. Still working with the National Gardens Scheme trying to persuade Cumbrian gardeners to open their gardens and trying to keep my own up to standard. Husband still involved with aged cars (although thank goodness he has given up racing them). This year we took his 1923 Bentley up to Skye with a group of like-minded friends, as well as a trip to France in a Jaguar. Saw **Jane Simpson (Witt)** this year who is now living in Somerset, also **Liz Constance** (can't for the life of me remember her married name!) Also see **Sue Coveney (Hyman)** when I am in London. She broke her hip in November and is still hobbling. She broke it falling in the underground which isn't the easiest place.

Joyce Seaman (Carnegie) Every year, when Julia writes asking for our news, I am reminded of a phrase taught to us by Miss Snow *in status quo*, as nothing seems to change from year to year. But at the same time I realise that in this unchanging state we are very fortunate, for a number of our friends are either struggling with debilitating ailments, or are not even with us anymore. However, another Westonbirt memory was an end of term report my parents received stating "she is untidy and forgetful". I am not proud of this but if, whoever it was who wrote that, thought I was forgetful then, what would she think NOW?!

One thing I do remember is that our son Alastair, has gone to Business School in New York and I think we may have lost him to the States with which he is, at the moment, completely enamoured.

Section 33 (1963)
Section Representative:
Helen Faircliff (Wienholt)

I have, unfortunately, to start with sad news and report the death of **Helen Danielsen (Davies)** who died on 24th October 2014 aged 69. Helen was in Beaufort and left WB in 1962. I wrote on your behalf to Helen's husband offering the condolences of our section.

Prue Bishop (Taylor) This year has been especially memorable as Claire Marshall spent a few days with us, and we had a lovely time together taking a look at various parts of Switzerland. Otherwise, I keep as active as I can, with a small amount of running together with some alpine and cross-country family skiing. In my studio the artwork continues to move ahead nicely.

Suzanne Burroughs (Bradbury) Still playing tennis, bridge and croquet with a lot of gardening also. My son Nicholas works for Stihl, and they are putting in a skywalk down at the Westonbirt Arboretum - could be interesting. He recently stayed at the Hare and Hounds and said it was excellent. A change from my memories of a rather dull and dowdy hotel.

Rosemary Connelly (Braddon) I'm in the process of giving up my beloved garden and downsizing to a condominium.

Susan Coveney (Hyman) Wonderful year enjoying two granddaughters who keep me on my toes. Also went to Naples and visited Denise Porter (now Deni Bittolo) and Gino, her very amusing Sicilian husband. Their first sightseeing excursion was to drive us around the outside of the Napoli football stadium at high speed. I had taken various Yorkshire food specialities, and we hope they will be in the UK later this year.

I have also seen **Helen Faircliff** and **Alannah Rylands (Hall)**, who continues to be the best gardener in Cumbria, and **Caroline Henderson (Beloe)** and **Julia Tingle** who are also very talented gardeners. I continue to hear from **Liz Morris**.

Anita Dudley (Armstrong) I am still living in Kuwait. Small pond so getting to be a bigger fish. Teaching English from pre-Level 1 to IELTS specialist and getting people immigration and university entrance qualifications. I never thought I would be a teacher (Miss Challen must be wondering!) but I really enjoy the satisfaction achieved!

My niece was married in a fabulous, Cheshire-style wedding in September. Two trips to Turkey for seaside rest - Gumbet near Bodrum - and also to visit the historical centre of Istanbul. If anyone needs a reasonable hotel in either place, I have them.

Otherwise no changes. The climate here is wonderful from mid-October to April, so anyone is welcome to visit - alcohol free, unfortunately. A bit of a difference from life in Mallorca!

Helen Faircliff (Wienholt) Thank you all for sending in your news year after year. Without it our section of the magazine would not exist, so it really is important. I continue to enjoy my retirement and volunteering with Riding for the Disabled, the Twickenham Museum and The National Archive. Also doing my genealogy research which is expanding with other people now asking for assistance, which is fun. My mother made 100 last July, and my son and I organised a party at her house. The Queen duly obliged with a birthday card. and she thoroughly enjoyed her day. Over the last year, I have seen, in no particular order, **Di Hughes, Susie Iliffe, Mandy Smith, Sue Hyman, Lin Maiden, Suz Bradbury, Prue Taylor** and **Anne Grocock**.

Sandra Russell (Morris) All well, thankfully. The Grim Reaper seems to be taking more from our pen these days, very sad.

All seven grandchildren keeping us happy and busy; all but one at school now. We take our turn in hols to help out working parents. Had great holiday to Faroes and Iceland last year; enjoyed it so much we are going again this year, taking in St Kilda islands as well. Also "bucket listed" Pompeii and Herculaneum in September for a week. The latter much more interesting.

Still busy with NADFAS and bridge club. Hillwalking is more long Glen walks these days. Awaiting the spring/summer for the garden again, too. We are very lucky to be near Edinburgh and Pitlochry for theatre and concert visits. Just seen the Turner Watercolours in the National Gallery, quite a revelation. The bequest states that they are only on show in January to protect them from harsh light. Also took in Castiglione drawings in Queen's Gallery at Holyrood.

Jane Simpson (Witt) We have been in our new house for just over a year and beginning to get it the way we like though still have plans for some building work. John has now fully recovered from his triple bypass operation last January and is a new man. We had our daughter Bryony's wedding here in July, just managing to squeeze the marquee into the garden. The weather was kind to us and we had wonderful caterers, which all helped to make the day a great success. Bryony is now expecting her first baby in June, which will be our fourth grandchild, so we are very excited. See if I manage to actually finish a bit of knitting for this one!

Jo Wilson (Forcey) now lives pretty close to us and we have managed to see each other twice this year and also seen **Liz Graley (Constance)** three times which has been great.

We are off to South America tomorrow on holiday, going on a cruise for the first time, visiting Brazil, Uruguay and Argentina and the highlight being a visit to the Rio Carnival.

Julia Tingle Retirement is turning out to be as busy for me as everyone else. Last year I changed guardian agencies and am much happier with the present one. If anyone is thinking of being a guardian, please email me, because they are always desperate for good guardians, and I could let you have any info you needed to aid consideration. It is not onerous, but you just need to set aside half terms to be in this country. Usually there are one or two exeats per term in addition to the child overnighting with you at the beginning and end of term. With G-Net you can even opt out of taking them to Heathrow, or meeting them at the airport, if it is a problem: I used to have to do this six times a year. There is a retainer, and expenses are paid promptly, unlike the previous agency. The children are mostly Japanese, very polite, and between the ages of 11 and 14 when they first come to a guardian. The sister of my present girl is actually at Westonbirt.

Rosemary Wolfe (Callard) 2014 saw me visiting Burma in February, Iceland (for the third tine) in May, and Turkey in October. I have now just returned from 17 days in Ecuador, visiting the Galapagos and Amazonia, which was all a wonderful experience.

I am still teaching music and have 16 pupils. I have seen **Wendy Firrell (Mathison)** and her new husband recently, and have been in contact with **Gill Jordan (Atkinson)** who sadly lost her father in January, and **Helen Bianchi (Fairbrother)**.

I keep very busy with local activities and play badminton, swim, walk, sing in a choir and go walking. A big birthday looms this year.

Apart from that, work continued in 2014 and the beginning of 2015 on trying to block the dreaded development 500 metres from me, which we have staved off for six years and got reduced in size twice. However, district councils these days seem to be intent on avoiding punitive costs by developers cashing in on every greenfield in the south, so sometimes inappropriate developments are waved through when they would have been deemed totally unacceptable only a few years ago. It is a constant David vs Goliath fight to preserve the countryside as the National Trust and CPRE are only too well aware. The Council for the Protection of Rural England did a wonderful job in supporting us. I am all for housing where needed, especially if the affordable housing element is in place, but what is hard to bear is that finally we lost the appeal recently to something which is not housing for the village, but an enormous cash-cow care-home for the developer, which will be plonked in entirely the wrong place, and will have a huge adverse environmental and traffic effect. So much for the Localism Bill.

On a happier note, a short holiday last September at a friend's villa in Minorca was an opportunity to sample some wonderful food and scenery. Pebbles, the Parsons Terrier, keeps me sane, as does being in the beautiful Sussex countryside for as long as it remains like that.

I always like getting emails from some of our group and hope to see **Jess** when she and her husband come to Glyndebourne this year. I hope all keep well in the coming year.

Anthea Shipley (Franklin-Adams) I lost my lovely horse Jake this time last year with colic and have now got a gypsy trotter that is lovely to drive but not so good to ride, so we will have to see!

I went to Iceland fishing with my husband, which was lovely and caught salmon, sea trout and char all on the same river.

Section 32 (1962)

Section Representative:
Sarah Rundle (Milner)

I am sure we will all be sad to hear of the death of **Charmian Reeve (Rooper)** who many of us will remember. On behalf of Section 32, sincere condolences to her family.

Helen Bianchi (Fairbrother) Still working as a GP Practice Pharmacist. I have an endless quest for knowledge, which Westonbirt inspired perhaps?

Looking back, we were so incredibly fortunate to have heard some of the great musical talent of the time, having no choice whether to attend probably widened most people's horizons. We all seemed to enjoy a varied selection of music - calypsos included I remember (with Pam Booth). Also having compulsory sport, certainly my trigger to improve was the thought of a decent team tea!

This past year I have seen **Gay Durston** - following the musical theme – we went to Neville Holt for a wonderful evening of *La Bohème* and a meal in the beautiful gardens, and then to London to see *Shakespeare in Love*; also another treat at Covent Garden this year. I have met up with **Casha Robertson** who was on her way to London, which was great after 30ish years.

Roe Callard and I make contact each year, and this year I am sure we shall meet up and also **Steph Judson**. We have had chats on the phone, especially when WB seemed to be on TV. I think the *Tatler* programme showed some footage, and also a TV film with Jane Seymour - suddenly Greg Wise appeared as a teacher in the fictional co-ed school (as if!)

Denise Bittolo (Porter) The event of the year for me was the short visit of **Sue (Hyman)** and her husband Michael. Sue and I actually began school together in Leeds at the age of five, and then continued on to Westonbirt. We had not seen each other for over 50 years, but recognized each other immediately at the airport! It was so nice seeing her after so long and wonderful to catch up on the news of old friends from WB. Sue keeps in touch with lots of people, whereas I have lost touch with everyone being so far away.

In September, Simone arrived on the scene, and we now have three grandsons, 6, 4 and 4 months. I have given up hope of ever going into a toyshop and buying a doll!

My husband was diagnosed with cancer and was operated on in October, but everything went well, and he is more or less back to normal. I still go for my six month check-ups with the 'oncologo', and so far, so good.

We will be coming over to the UK this year finally. The last time I was over was when my mother passed away which was 18 years ago. No excuse at all, I know.

Elizabeth Bryant Most of this year seem to have been spent trying to make my house wind and water-tight after ghastly weather last year. I had the scaffolding taken down yesterday after eight weeks, and the house is much lighter as a result. I'm still enjoying living in Bradford on Avon. There's plenty to do here, and it's not far from Bath. I went to *War Horse* at the Bristol Hippodrome last week. I was lucky to get tickets at all, but was not impressed by how hard the (bench) seats were in the Gods. Bath Theatre Royal is far more civilised!

I've had quite a few friends staying this year and visited friends in Bavaria and Denmark. I belong to a couple of walking groups and help organise the Walking Festival here in September. I've booked a walking holiday in Sardinia for May, and may go to Brunei and Malaysia later in the year.

Carolyn Henson (Iliffe) I am living in North Yorkshire on the edge of the Wolds, and not far from the coast. This is a lovely place to live in semi-retirement. I completed work as Chaplain at Saint Michael's Hospice at Harrogate a few years ago, and continue to have some ministry in this large parish, where there are eight rural churches. I have a private practice as a psychotherapist - work which I have been doing for many years now after training in London, Nottingham and Sheffield.

My two sons have a total of 12 children between them, and two of my grandchildren each have a son, giving me two great-grandchildren, and a third is due quite soon. I see my two sisters, Jennie and Susie, quite often. Last year we went to Italy together with my brother-in-law, John. We had a lovely holiday to celebrate my 70th Birthday. This year will be Jennie's 70th, and we are all getting together in the USA, where Jennie and John live, and spending some time in Florida on an island in the Gulf of Mexico. We shall be surrounded by warm seas in Jennie's dream birthday venue!

I have planted a lovely garden around my present home and look forward to more planting this spring. I also play the piano and continue to practise and try to improve my playing. I am just a little bit better now than in my last year at Westonbirt. I shall always be grateful for a good musical education at Westonbirt. This is one thing that still stands me in good stead.

Jyotipakshini (Erica Harding) Things are jogging along quite well at present. I turned 70 in October and decided that now I'd had my three score years and ten, I'd let go a few aspects of my life and move on. So I've resigned from a couple of charity committees where I was a trustee and retired from some of the meditation teaching I was doing at the Glasgow Buddhist Centre. I'm still keeping on with the Breathworks Mindfulness for Stress and Mindfulness for Health Courses which I run. I find them stimulating and a challenge; the feedback we get shows that they seem to have a very positive effect on those who come. Hopefully though some younger people in Glasgow will train to run these courses before too long.

I now have five grandchildren, three are local and two in Yorkshire. I love being with them, but realise how I'm ageing when I recall that I coped with three small children, a full-time job, a dog and house to maintain every day - and even woke up each morning feeling refreshed! I'm sure lots of you may feel the same.

Next Monday, Michael and I are off to Australia and Papua New Guinea for a couple of months. We both have cousins in Aussie, so the excuse is that we are going to see them, which we will. However we've both only been to Australia once before and loved it, so we are going again before we feel too old for the long plane journey.

Which reminds me that I was on a long retreat on my birthday, so I am having a delayed party in May. This is taking the form of a samba drumming workshop with enough instruments for everyone and equally suitable (I hope) for grandchildren, our children in their forties, friends of various ages and grannies! So far people have responded to their invitations with great enthusiasm, so I'm keeping my fingers crossed that all will go well.

Sarah Rundle (Milner) Firstly, once again, thank you to everyone who replied to my request for news, and good to hear from them the news of others.

My life this year has been much the same as last, and it goes so fast. Robin is battling with Parkinson's, but he doesn't let that stop him doing all he wants to do. His cancer is stable at present.

I had a second knee replacement in September – same knee - two half knee replacements now on each side. I gather it isn't done very often, but it does mean that you keep the middle bit of your knee. So far very successful, and I am out walking again properly. Had our usual visits to Wimbledon and the tennis at the O2 and two glorious weeks in Perthshire in July. When we were in London, we fitted in a visit to the Rembrandt Exhibition at the National Gallery and the moving display of poppies at The Tower of London.

Have just returned from visiting our youngest daughter, Nicola, and her family near Toulouse. They were here in the summer when we had a family gathering for the baptism of two of our grandchildren. Ella, who is ten, hadn't been baptised as they live in France so she joined Iver, who is a year old. The wonderful and most memorable part of the service for me was that Ella replaced our usual organist and played the organ for us – she has a wonderful teacher in France and we were so proud of her. It was lovely to have all the family and all the grandchildren (who range from 18 months to 18 years) together, it doesn't happen very often. We do see quite a lot of Claire and her boys as they are in Bristol and have seen more of Jon and family now they have moved from Scotland to Oxford. A very different life for them, and I am horrified at their childcare costs.

As I write, Caerhays Castle and Gardens have just opened and we are both working there again. Very much a spring garden, so they only open until June. I never tire of walking around the gardens with the dogs in the early evening after the gardens have closed.

Liz Bryant and I still communicate by email and put the world to rights together, and it is lovely to hear from **Deb Soper** again. I think some of us are 70 this year. Where on earth have all those years gone?

Deborah Soper I took the car over to Dartmoor at the end of May, hoping to look up childhood haunts and do some painting. I didn't do much of the latter as it was mostly not warm and dry enough to sit about outside. I did however manage a first visit to Wistman's Wood and painted an image of the stunted moss-covered oaks and boulders there, really enjoyed finding and admiring the old places and stayed nearly two weeks in an excellent little cottage. Managed to eschew too much cream!

In August I joined in a brilliant painting course near Wheatley run by **Margaret Merritt**, always a lot of fun and tremendously stimulating. My sister came too and we had fun finding a different place to eat each night.

In September I visited my littlest grandchild in Shrewsbury, and as I see her so rarely it was a real treat. Then I went on to Leeds, where my sister and I joined a group looking at twentieth century art in Yorkshire, a good museum in Leeds and Hockney, Moore and Hepworth, among others, elsewhere. Then we had a couple of days in York, which I rather fell in love with. Back in Cirencester with my sister, I organised an impromptu 50th anniversary for our matriculation with Oxford Zoology contemporaries, including **Carolyn Halliday (Wheeler)**. **Sue Whitfield (Bottomley)** swelled our numbers so the score was Oxford 6, Cambridge 1, Westonbirt 3 (some interesting overlaps there!) We had a great reunion at Westonbirt Arboretum, including lunch outside and proper English 'champagne' - what a great hobby for retirement!

After all that travelling, I decided to hunker down here in Guernsey for a few months. I have been painting bays of Guernsey, mostly in the more clement months, and 14 down still have quite a few to do, as well as other subjects. Like lots of you, we benefit here from live broadcasts from the National Theatre and ROH, and there is a decent concert hall here, not confined to local instrumentalists. It all helps one get through the winter!

Susan Whitfield (Bottomley) Life bowls along, with a new grandchild in France bringing the total to nine. There will be a great gathering in April when our son gets married near Bath, and no doubt at least a thousand photos will be taken.

I went on the very interesting Old Girls' trip to Highgrove Garden and lunch in the spring, and greatly recommend it if you like looking at gardens. The lunch was delicious, and there were some very healthy plants for sale too.

On a sunny day in early autumn, I met up with a group of friends based around St Anne's College Oxford in 1964 entry for zoology, at the arboretum. This had been organised by **Deb Soper**, and **Carolyn Wheeler** was the other ex WB member of the group. I know another member of the group very well, and as we live nearby, I went as an honorary Oxford zoologist, despite having been to Cambridge. Although I have seen Deb a few times in recent years, I had not seen Carolyn for many a long decade, so it was great to see them again.

My fourth daughter currently works for DFID in Islamabad, so Robert and I went there last April to visit her, and were able to go to Lahore and Taxila. The security situation is such that roaming free can get complicated but we thoroughly enjoyed what we could do. I have had secondhand connections with Pakistan on and off all my life, so it was a real treat to visit even a few places. Taxila has the ruins of civilisations from the Greeks onwards, covering many religions including Zoroastrian, Buddhist and Christian, and at least one building had elements remaining from each of these. In time, no doubt it will become a popular tourist destination for foreigners.

I am still a governor at Westonbirt, and greatly enjoy visiting the school. It has been much improved with recent investments and some other changes, and the atmosphere is very happy among boarders and day girls alike. The prep school is also flourishing, using the buildings we knew as the San and staff house, as well as many of the senior school facilities where appropriate.

The Italian and other gardens are being improved all the time (by a separate charity, The Holfords of Westonbirt Trust), and are open to visitors on Wednesdays - well worth checking times and visiting if you are going near, for a very beautiful nostalgia trip.

Maybe I was just a bit vague, but I was not remotely aware as a pupil that we had a double-decker pond, with what had originally been (and is now again) a glass side wall to the top one so you can see the fish. This has now been totally restored at great cost, donated by a wealthy philanthropist who liked ponds, and is very splendid indeed. It is quite a rarity if not actually unique.

Gay Woodley (Durston) My year has been much the same as before: lots of visits to South Wales to see/babysit the grandchildren, now all at one or other of the Monmouth Schools. We went to see Maya play lax against Westonbirt in November, only her second match, as it ia a club sport only at her school, and Haberdashers won! I was fully expecting WB to win. Then went to the Winter Walk at the Arboreteum in the evening, which was magical and I would recommend it, the trees were lit up in beautiful different colours and there were lots of interesting ways to light various areas.

We took the family to North Norfolk this summer, had wonderful weather, played tennis (court behind our rented house), and spent several days on Wells and Brancaster beaches without the North wind - remarkable!

We went to Malta, Crete and Croatia, absolutely beautiful cruise on a small boat able to go into the most charming and interesting little ports and harbours as well as the very popular Split and Dubrovnik, where we stayed on for two extra days in order to see a bit more of the town in our own time.

I took Maya (then 11) to Florence for a few days in April,where we looked at Michelangelo's David and the half-finished sculptures in detail. We found an excellent children's guide to the town, and it made us look up and go all over the place. She loved the whole experience including proper Italian pasta. At last I managed to go up the Leaning Tower of Pisa which has always been closed for restoration before.

In July, Paul's Mother was a hundred, so we organised a party in the garden with all her children, grand and great grand children. She was very pleased with her card from the Queen and coped with the festivities very well.

I have just "celebrated" my 70th birthday. I can't quite believe it! My daughter and family gave me a gorgeous leather jacket, so I am not allowed to act my age!

Have seen **Helen Bianchi** several times over the year. We go to the opera and concerts together, which is lovely.

Section 31 (1961)

Section representative:
Priscilla Llewelyn (Rickard)

Judith Evans (Beesly) We had a busy 2014. Family arriving for weekend stays – five grandchildren ages 6 down to 3. We have three girls and two boys, all very robust and full of character! Great holiday in Menorca with friends, calm before the storm. We drove down to Provence and had a wonderful two weeks in a rented house with all three children plus little ones, and still space for friends too. Bad weather first week and great second week! We do Marlborough Summer School every year. A fantastic array of courses to choose from – family staying again. I had a hip replacement in October – very successful – followed by exercises to the letter. 70th Birthday in December!

Penny Faust (Posner) I can hardly say that the past couple of years have been quiet. After nearly 40 years in the same place, I have moved house. After Wilfred died, I was very conscious that the house was too big for one person, but it took me a long time to let go. I finally had it valued by three separate agents, who all came up with the same price but were very different in their response to my need to find somewhere else to live. One found a bungalow that was well out of my price range. The second said that it was surprising how selling my house would focus my mind on finding somewhere else - daft really because if he didn't understand that a single woman in her late 60s was not going to cast herself adrift without somewhere else to go, then he was not the man for me! And the third listened carefully to what I said, and 24 hours later phoned me to say that he had been approached by a young man who was converting a small bungalow into a 3 bed chalet bungalow backing on to Bury Knowle Park in Headington itself.

To cut a long story short, I went along to have a look, met the builder, took a month to make up my mind and then put the house on the market. Selling houses now is very different from the last time I did it, and I found the bidding process quite exciting! The most difficult aspect of moving was what to do with my books. I've collected books ever since I was about 8, never letting any go, but I managed to give away about half; the criterion for retention was whether I would ever read the book again. And of course there was the detritus of 40 years to be cleared!

I found it very exhilarating and energising making decisions about the new house all the way through the conversion/building process, and now I have what I want, including the potential to live downstairs should I no longer feel comfortable climbing stairs, not imminent I can assure you.

The house is five minutes across the Park from Headington itself, London buses and easy access to the city. And I can still have one family at a time to stay. The move was far less stressful than I had anticipated - I was obviously really ready to go. The dog was very peeved about it, he didn't eat for three days, but now recognises that he still has a (smaller) garden to prowl round, and being next to the Park has distinct advantages. So far, so good.

The family are all busy and doing well. In 2013 my eldest son was given a personal Chair by Southampton University and is now Professor of Paediatric Infectious Diseases. Wilfred would have been beside himself with pride, and I confess that I went into stereotypical Jewish mother mode! There are now 21 of us when we all get together - my 12th grandchild was born recently - and we had a wonderful party on my 70th birthday in October 2014. The children are all growing fast and seem to approve of the new house, especially the eaves cupboards for hide and seek, and its proximity to the Park which has great facilities for both older and younger children. 'Grandma duty' takes up quite a lot of my time, especially driving round the countryside to catch up with them all.

I am still very much involved in interfaith work and am currently Chair of the Oxford Council of Faiths and jointly responsible for the annual Inter-Faith Friendship Walk. This takes place every June on a route which goes from the Synagogue to the Central Mosque, stopping at various churches in the City on the way. If you live in the Oxford area do join us!

Sue Garden, Baroness Garden Of Frognal (Button) After a more flexible year on the back benches, I was reappointed to be a Government Whip/Spokesperson and Baroness-in-Waiting in November. This time I lead on Women and Equalities, and support Education and DEFRA. I was delighted to be involved with the Women Bishops' Bill and look forward to seeing women on the Bishops' benches in the Lords. As I write in February, the Election is an unknown quantity. In the Lords, we know we'll be back, and that Liberal Democrats will play a significant part, but it will be up to the electorate whether we are in Government or in Opposition!

Business travels included my first visit to Japan for the UK-Japan 21st century group conference in Tokyo and Hakone, an unforgettable experience; a visit to Airbus in Toulouse; and another to the Catalan government in Barcelona to find out more about their bid for independence.

One daughter is COO for Solent NHS Trust, the other a primary school teacher. One son-in-law runs a micro-brewery, the other runs scripted TV comedy for Freemantle. The four grandchildren are doing well at school and with myriad other activities. I continue to be involved with the World Traders' Livery Company, the War Widows' Association, modern languages, Hampstead Church, the Air League, and enjoy keeping up with family and friends.

Stephanie Grant (James) It was lovely to meet up with **Sarah Bays (Fisher)** for a lunch and reminisce about school, family and friends. Time rushes by, but we still had a lot in common and laughed at the same things. It was the big '7-0' birthday last year, but we will celebrate the event this Easter by taking all the family to Brittany. Next year John and I will celebrate our 50th wedding anniversary - how incredible is that!

Priscilla Llewelyn (Rickard) My family continues to expand. My youngest daughter (a past WB pupil) has a baby boy, and in total I now have eight grandchildren. I can remember their names but not all their birthdays now. I have had a particularly busy year at Penpergwm House, the residential home that I have been running for 28 years. A new extension has finally risen from the ground. and we are now hoping to gain nursing status for some rooms in the home. It's lovely collating all the news, thank you so much to all in my Section for sending it in to me, and please keep sending!

Jane Merritt (Wilkinson) Life continues to be very busy. I am starting my second year as Senior Warden of Christ Episcopal Church in New Bern, NC. We are celebrating our 300th Anniversary this year, with many activities planned throughout the year. Lord and Lady Carey (former Archbishop of Canterbury) and Bishop Mike Hill of Bristol are among our special guests. We are about to call a new Rector for our Parish, which is most exciting.

Last year, my grandson was confirmed in Copenhagen in May, so I had the privilege of attending and giving a talk at the dinner following. I returned to Denmark in August with Keith, and we stayed at Michael's summer house in Hornbaek. It is delightfully relaxing to be with the family and away from the busyness of church! Keith and I spent a week in DC sightseeing and visiting Keith's family, and then we had a relaxing week on the Outer Banks of NC after Christmas, enjoying the deserted beaches. It is a perfect place to run! Yes, I have not given that up yet, but the pace is slower!

I enjoy reading the newsletters and the Old Girls' news. I am made aware of my age when I now have to go to the back of the Association News to find our Section! I feel very blessed to have good health, a wonderful family, and a fulfilling life in the church and at the prisons we visit.

Jane Mounsey (Bennion) This is an advertisement! I have a holiday cottage in Pembrokeshire (where I was brought up) which is wonderfully comfortable, sleeps eight, five minutes' (possibly three minutes' depending on how fast you walk!) walk to the beach, beautiful coastal paths, blissful countryside. For availability, prices and other info, see *www.carewcottage.com*. Not much other news – luckily I am healthy and have a healthy husband. Long may that last.

Jenny Reid (Reid) On retirement from two careers, first as a teacher of German and EFL in Yorkshire and then London, second as a town planner in London, I retired with my partner to the North Pennines. Here I resumed my longstanding enjoyment of ceramics and also started painting. I mostly do abstracts and semi-abstracts in pastels or acrylics but recently attempted watercolours, without much success! I've sold a few pieces at local exhibitions.

I also enjoy photography and love gardening, but that is quite a challenge up here. I sing in a community choir and go to a yoga group followed by coffee and scones and a good chat. With local friends I see films and have benefitted greatly from the live streamings of theatre, opera and ballet. Owning a springer spaniel ensures that I walk every day in the lovely Pennines.

I still travel quite a bit. Last year to Turkey for an annual activity holiday, then Andalucia. and most years we spend a month or so in our family farmhouse in the north of Scotland. Occasionally I stay in London and have an orgy of galleries etc as well as catching up with London friends. Sometimes I manage to see **Sally Fletcher** and **Sue (now Lady) Garden**. I seem to have lost touch with anyone else from WB, but would love to hear from anyone I might have known.

Gillian Wynes (Ross Goobey) My son and his family visited from America last August. My son, Anthony, was over here to swim in Loch Lomond for "The Big Swim". It was lovely to see them, and how the children (George, 12, and Millie, 9) have grown up. My other children and grandchildren are fine. I'm still going dancing every week, it's good exercise. I had one night in London, when we went to my great niece's naming ceremony in August.

Section 30 (1960)
Section Representative:
Jane Reid (Bottomley)

You will be sad to hear that **Ann Bament (Best)** died around Christmas 2014. We send our condolences to her family.

Phoebe Field (Northcroft) I have enjoyed seeing the progress of our grandson's first year of life, and look forward to the second. How did we manage? Amnesia is a blessing at times. More planting last winter/spring, but it has been a very dry spring/summer, so we are hoping for rain asap this autumn. I have seen **Maggie Rhys-Jones (Hughes)** on two short occasions during her latest trip, also **Pat Davidson (Weaver)**, our contemporary, but not an Association member, for whom lack of rain had not been good this year, after wind storms for a tidy up and to deliver wood. I have corresponded with **Jenny Greatwood (Bawtree)** who has had a worrying and frustrating year.

The ancestor collection continues with great interest, and the general election added a noisy interlude. The cricket World Cup is entertaining at present - nice to be playing at home for our team. Best wishes to all our Section, wherever you are.

Jenny Greatwood (Bawtree) This year has been rather different for me. Great start to the year with visit to grandchildren in SA. Then colourful week in Morocco buying up the souks with my sister-in-law. Then a brief visit to Finland with my sister Sally to see the Northern Lights, with daytime husky driving, snowmobiling and cross country skiing.

While doing the skiing on the last day I managed to fall over onto solid ice and knocked myself out. Seeming okay, I skied on, and we flew back as planned the next day. Sally (in her nursing mode) insisted I went to the GP before she drove back home to Devon. Doc sent me for MRI scan - deemed to be fine. Five days later, I flew out to South Africa again and had a great time cycling etc with the kids.

Only after I returned did I start to have problems - driving, balance etc. To cut long story short: on June 21st I ended up in QE Birmingham having brain surgery. Very successful and brilliant care, unfortunately then suffered very minor seizures which they deemed to be mild epilepsy. This meant I can't drive for a whole year! Nightmare, as no access to buses and have to get a lift to everywhere. But I have to remind myself I am otherwise very well. I am now allowed to do anything I want - except drive. So frustrated, but very lucky and counting the days till June 26th when hopefully I will get my licence back.

I am also in touch with **Sarah Blizzard (Gardiner), Pepi Cowell (Bowring), Phoebe Field** and **Linda Morley** (both **Northcroft**).

Anna Ingledew (Williams) We carry along just a little slower. I have Hepatitis C, so don't know how much longer I shall last. The NHS kindly donated it to me in a blood transfusion 30 years ago. However we now have four grandchildren, aged three and under, who give us lots of fun and pleasure.

Felicity Macdonald (Northcote) Strange that, although usually very busy, I seem to have very little to report. Maybe that is because I am doing much the same as before and have reported it all in previous years. Lay Ministry and other church commitments are interesting and mostly enjoyable, but incredibly time-consuming. Domestically there always seems something to be done, and I enjoy spending time with nearby family members. Recently I have become involved on a purely voluntary basis with a new, local, project for children with special needs - I'm learning a lot. With my little dog in tow, I continue to make regular visits to a delightful village inn in Yorkshire. I hope to attend the reunion at WB this year. Health pretty good, but I do run out of energy at times - getting older. Best wishes to you all.

Carol Mullin (Rostron) This year my one-year old grandson's parents have removed him to Perth, Oz. I'd been lucky enough to spend a lot of time minding him over the last 10 months, so missing him badly. I am off to visit them all in March. Exciting! I'm still doing spasmodic work as an illustrator. That's fun too.

Juliet Peel (De Galleani) We have moved to the centre of Bakewell.

Jane Reid (Bottomley) My husband has been working towards giving up work at the end of September 2015. I see his retirement as an opportunity for clearance of innumerable boxes of paper from his past; the next generation (who live three hours journey away) see it as an opportunity for school holiday child-care problems to be over. I rather have the feeling that his own dreams of how to fill his days are different!

Rosemary Somers (Fuchs-Marx) Thanks to Tony's continued remission, we have had a good year. I have had minor surgery on my lower left eyelid, so no longer had an itchy eye nor a bag under it! We strive to maintain our health by continuing our diet and exercise routines – tennis, body conditioning and, in my case, Latin dancing. Professionally, Tony does a little legal work to keep his brain ticking over, advising a barrister colleague of his. He also studies the shrinking ice-caps and sunspots on the internet to keep track of climate change! For my part, I have done a little voluntary teaching at the local primary school, which I have much enjoyed. It was rewarding when the children made me a lovely thank you card. I have also done a bit of handwriting tuition at home. Our Lib Dem political interests continue, as does our solid contact with the family, especially the grandchildren.

Sallie Sullivan (Sanderson) I am very busy, still working, teaching yoga and training teachers. Four grandkids!

Of those that did not send news as such: **Lesley Godwin (Neill)** won't make it to this year's reunions. **Bodhiniya (Ann Udal)** and **Janetta Looker (Webb**, now retired from the Association) have also said that they won't be coming. **Avril Goldstein (Le Tissier), Jeannie Astill (Mackenzie), Joan Madonko (Scott)** plan to come, and **Penny Cowell (Bowring)** and **Lisi Reisz** are thinking about it.

Section 29 (1959)
Section Representative:
Angela Fenhalls (Allen)

Julie Ann Anley (Julie Wilson) is back in touch thanks to Myrth Russell. Julie says that last year their family ancestral home burnt down as a result of an electrical fault. Luckily no-one was hurt, and furniture and pictures were saved. Julie's second daughter, Marion is living in the USA, owns the house, garden, lake and adjoining fields, and is battling with insurers in the High Court. Julie lives across the river from Mourne Park House, her elder daughter Bonnie and three children live the other side of the mountains of Mourne, and Phillip, a teacher with two children, lives in Cirencester. Phillip and his wife are restoring The Old School House beside Julie's cottage.

Nonie Beckingsale (Joan Hills) The Beckingsales celebrated their Golden Wedding Anniversary last August with a large family party.They have six grandchildren who are all doing well. A largish house and garden reveal the need for attention to hip problems, and they hope solutions are not too long delayed. Nonie says it can take time in Wales but the care is excellent when it comes. She still runs the church choir and Mike has handed on the chairmanship of the British Legion.

Angela Fenhalls (Allen) We took the plunge and downsized to Kew eight years ago. I resented the idea initially, but have been proven wrong. Our son and family live close by, near enough for the two grandchildren to drop in on the way home from school. Kew Gardens, where I am a tour guide, is a source of joy; friends and things botanical. Our daughter takes possession of a derelict small holding in West Wales at the end of March; a dream I can understand, though it will be a considerable challenge for her. I hope to drop in on Nonie *en route* to see her. If anyone fancies a walk (and talk) in Kew Gardens I would love to see you.

Libby Houston We had a long chat on the phone after Juliet's death, recalling when we three had shared a room in the sixth form. Libby continues to pursue her botanical interests in North Somerset and is much admired for her work by senior botanists at Kew Gardens.

Linda Morley (Northcroft) is finding that her lovely house and garden seem to get bigger! Two choral societies take up much of her time. She sang Mozart's Requiem in Naples last spring and has sung in several local concerts. She is no longer involved in mainstream politics, but remains a member of the European Union of Women. She continues to collect fans and will help organise the International AGM meeting in Cheltenham next year. She has a daughter Sarah and a son Jeremy, with two daughters, who is currently planning a job change.

Myrth Russell (Hudson) Myrth has recently joined the Association - only just after me! She moved to Scotland with her second husband almost 20 years ago. He was an engineer, and before retiring they ran a sail loft on the West Coast. They also owned a ladies' shoe shop in Helensburgh. Myrth still plays chamber music with occasional concerts, and they sail, walk and dance. She would like to be in touch again with old friends.

Juliet Townsend (Smith) very sadly died last November. National obituaries paid tribute to a remarkable career of service including her role as Lord Lieutenant of Northamptonshire from 1998 to June, 2014. Her appointment made her the first woman to take the title since its creation 450 years ago.

Section 28 (1958)
Section Representative:
Milada Haigh (Weir)

It's noticeable that our generation of Westonbirt survivors seems to be mainly winding down as everyday life gets more difficult, but that only highlights the brave souls who determinedly buck the trend.

Sheila Astbury (Stuart) I'm just about to go to Sri Lanka. Last year it was South Africa in the winter, a walking holiday in Wengen in the Swiss mountains in the summer, and then a trip to the southern Peloponnese in the autumn. Travelling is one of the luxuries of retirement. Otherwise I remain the local organist, enjoy being a granny, and keep in touch with **Sue Hicks** and **Anne** and **Susan Mercer**.

Sue Hicks (Harker) In March we celebrated John's 75th birthday by travelling to Brussels on Eurostar and having an interesting weekend in a hotel near the European Parliament, visiting the town and seeing some of the sights. The downside was having his iphone stolen at a café, and it took about a month to sort out the insurance. One becomes very dependent on these things, even addicted to them, but fortunately I still had my phone with most of the information on it.

April found me in Dundalk, Ireland, with Rosemary (our younger daughter) and her husband and four sons for a few days. We had fun and went for some beautiful forest walks.

In September John and I spent a week at an agriturismo farm above Lake Garda exploring the area, culminating in an amazing performance of *Aida* in Verona under a harvest moon.

It was our turn to entertain everybody at Christmas, and we had many visitors and celebratory meals, including a delightful couple from Poland who were staying with us.

We are thankful to be in good health, as far as we know. John still continues to do some tree work for our son-in-law, and I spend time on various U3A activities such as book club, walking, going to the theatre and visiting gardens (sometimes with **Sheila Astbury (Stuart)**, and conversing in French. Every so often I meet **Rowena Ginns (Cullin)** in Market Harborough for lunch and a chat. I am beginning to feel the need to fit as much as I can into whatever time we have left!

Anne Mercer (Seear) The big event of 2014 was Bill's 80th birthday at the beginning of December, when he was overwhelmed by receiving 94 cards as well as a party and a professional photograph to commemorate it.

Margaret Squires (Renshaw) We are slowing down in our aim to bag all the "relative hills of Britain" since someone else has bagged the St Kilda sea stacks, and from his account we know we are incapable of it. My own collection now stands at 1348 out of 1556, and those hills will probably last my walking lifetime, given my annual rate is now down to around 70 per annum. Our grandson is currently living with us as a student at St Andrews University.

Sue Bowden (Humpidge) I am still enjoying the country scene at Washbrook Cottage. accompanied by our donkeys, hens, sheep and

Shetland ponies. The grandchildren - both lots fortunately live nearby – love it here too.

It was exciting to witness a meet of the Beaufort hounds at the School recently; I don't remember that in our day. The school provided delicious refreshments for all.

I bumped into **Helen Var Ziliotis (Boyce)** on Reading station quite by chance. She was returning from Canada to visit her mother, aged 101! We hadn't met for nearly 50 years.

I have met up with **Libby Houston** and **Caroline Price** this year, most recently when we travelled to **Juliet Townsend (Smith)**'s memorial service in Northampton, together with **Lin Coleman (Hutton)**. It was a magnificent and memorable service, but a sad day. We all shared a dormitory in Badminton house.

Kate Whittingham (Norman-Moses) I would like to have more really good news. John and I are well or as well as anyone is at our age. We are coping with looking after a daughter with schizoaffective disorder who is living in a group home, and are parents to her daughter who is struggling with anorexia. So the planned retirement of travel and leisure is not happening. However, our granddaughter is a wonderful girl and we are happy to do it, although bringing a teenager up today is so different from 30 years ago! The other half of the family is doing well although they live on the other side of the country in Alberta, four hours by plane. We will be in the UK in July for a family reunion bringing all the grandchildren, which will be fun.

Paula Bradfield (Stovold) I have been suffering from various ailments - not mortal, just inconvenient. My eldest grandson, studying Greek and Chinese at Manchester, is preparing to spend the next academic year in Beijing. Paula is anxious about the poisonous air. Her daughter, with two toddlers, has abandoned the financial world and started fostering instead.

Ann Hildred (Jenkins) I seem to be getting into true retirement at last – still playing badminton and gardening, but am off the committee of the gardening club for the first time in 40 years and looking forward to a tourist trip to Canada in the autumn.

Penelope Jepson I am very pleased with the result of my first cataract operation, I can now see that my nightie is blue and white rather than dirty blue and yellow. Another plus is that my usual winter SAD (seasonal affective disorder) has much improved because more light is getting into my eyes! The one slightly odd thing is that having been short-sighted all her life, I would rather stay that way for ease of sewing and embroidery, which I do a lot.

Elizabeth Blood (Plant) Time goes too quickly! The grandchildren are growing up. One grandson plays rugby and cricket for Kent (under 13). A granddaughter plays hockey for Kent (under15). Just had a lovely holiday in Tanzania, half safari then beach in Zanzibar.

Jennie Bland (May) Another grandchild - 15 now. Happy family holidays with all, in our electricity-and-telephone-free lodge in wild part of north west Sutherland - fishing, cutting turf, puffin-watching etc then, with oil lamps, endless, noisy, board and card games. Perfect!

Christopher published his first novel, aged 76, to fantastic critical acclaim, but with predictably moderate book sales, though the Kindle sales have now reached 14,000!) Do get a copy: *Ashes in the Wind* by Christopher Bland, published by Head of Zeus. He's now working on his second, about the thirteenth-century repression of the Cathars.

My four older Byng children batter on - William working with his church, Georgie bringing out the movie of one of her Molly Moon books, Tara restoring an Irish house, Jamie publishing and working with World Book Night and the 'Letters Live' performances with Benedict Cumberbatch. My youngest, Archie Bland, is now with the *Guardian*, where he edits the Monday edition and writes occasional pieces.

I am still very involved with the Holfords of Westonbirt Trust. We are currently applying to the HLF for £1.35m to help with completing the garden restoration. Much has been done already including impressive work on the double pond. Do come to see it, and do please help with the funding!

Kate Smith (Maryrose "Buddy" Hammer) I planned to come to the reunion last year, but was frustrated by my husband's medical problems. Let's hope for better luck another time.

Milada Haigh (Weir) My news looks a lot like last year's. Looking forward to ending some more chemotherapy, and hoping nothing interferes with a hoped-for trip to Prague. Last year's visit did come off, by the way. Apart from that, I can report only that my grandson has achieved his mission in life, as foretold on the day of his birth. The size of his feet clearly showed a future policeman. His police training started in January.

Section 27 (1957)
Section Representative:
Angela Potter (Tracy)

This year has been a very sad one for those of us who knew **Sue Powell (Watkins)**. It was terrible watching her slow decline with Motor Neurone Disease. Right to the end (September 30th 2014), she was cheerful and positive, even though she could hardly move, and hadn't been able to communicate except through her iPad for nearly two years. The imminent birth of their first grandson kept her going, and she died soon afterwards. Her memorial service was beautifully done, with a delightful tribute and a rendering of 'If you knew Susie'. It was good to see **Oriel Rogers Coltman (Corbett)** for the first time is nearly 60 years! I had many emails from those of you in my two sections who remembered her with affection, as well as from **Naz Ashraf (Ikramullah)**, **Priscilla Hilton (Manser)** and **Pasty Fou (Toh)**. Thank you. One of the people I expected to see at her funeral, **Paddy Scott Clark (Angus)**, died very unexpectedly virtually on the same day, and I found myself representing the Westonbirt Association exactly two weeks later in the same church.

Very sadly there has been another death from our year group, and I will start this year's news with a lovely tribute from **Margaret Blackburn (Taylor)**:

"On December 29th I lost my oldest and dearest friend, **Margaret Niewland (Alexander)**. We had met aged 12 in January 1959 in the Lower IV form room at Westonbirt. We shared a common bond, which we wanted to keep a secret from everyone - Northumberland. She came from Black Hall, Ridley and I from Wooler (later Elsdon), near Newcastle to come to school in the south west. The north east had been badly bombed at the end of the war, and it was considered best for us to be educated in the south. No motorways, no Royals, and a long journey (it would take two days by car), which began at Newcastle Central at 8am, with our Mille Renée in charge (we did play her up!). After years in Badminton House, (I was in Beaufort), where Auntie Ayres looked after her asthma, Maggie left for a flat in Florence, where she learnt Italian, followed by a job in Tripoli. We were both drawn back north with husbands and children; Margaret's daughter Rosy still lives at Black Hall with her family. My girls were at Elsdon for a good part of their childhood holidays so there were many shared excursions and treasure hunts. She was the kindest person I have known. When my mother died she cooked meals for Pa and took them to him. I have really been blessed with such a friendship. RIP."

Now to more cheerful news. I'm delighted to welcome **Barbara Anderson** into Section 27. Barbara, although in the same year as me, had been in Section 25 because she left in 1955. Contemporaries will remember her as **Tucker Anderson** – she reverted to her first Christian name on her 21st birthday! She writes: 'I am now 75, and am fortunate to still be very well. I work at a charity, Hope and Homes for Children, for two half days/week. Having hardly written anything in more than note form since I left school (I was a doctor) I decided to join a U3A Creative Writing group. I also did a Writing course last year, and experienced red rings round my incorrect punctuation for the first time since Miss Warburton's classes more than 60 years ago. I occasionally meet up with **Janet Mccrae (Gregory)** for a country walk, and see **Gillie Drake (Strain)** when she and Nicholas come over from Guernsey. (I got to know Gillie when we were in the San with chickenpox at the same time!)

Joan Allan (Blakeborough) Our youngest, Colin (who is with BP), and his family arrived in Azerbaijan in August for a three or four year posting. They all appear to be settling in remarkably well and have come here for half term. The school seems to be considerably better than the local primary was in Torphins, Aberdeenshire, and that always helps. An added bonus is that Tessa, aged 4½, was able to start school, whereas in Scotland she would not start until next August (as the cut-off date in Scotland is end March and her birthday is 6th April).

Emily Bilmes (Rawlence) has advanced Parkinsons. She is unable to communicate and has limited mobility, so I was glad to hear from her sister, **Elizabeth Ells (Rawlence)**, that she has devoted carers and is still able to live in her flat overlooking Clapham Common, and retains a sense of humour. Sadly, her youngest sister, Mary, has MS and is also increasingly handicapped.

Judith Briggs (Walker) continues to live in Johannesburg with quite enough garden to keep them busy, and though the dog they had is no more, they still have a cat. She keeps busy with various local activities, a Residents Action Group, and helping to run a small project to assist the homeless in their area, as well as keeping involved with the local committee of the opposition political party, the Democratic Alliance. The government is less than efficient, especially at local level, so everyone hopes for a change. She continues to visit the Cape two or three times a year, with son, Guy, and family down there (though work brings him up to them quite often.) They had a lovely visit to the family in America last summer with a quick stop in London with sister Ann on the way home. Otherwise they remain pretty well and enjoy getting out and about. They had a lovely celebration for their Golden Wedding last December both at home in Johannesburg and then a repeat in Cape Town. They hope to get to the US again later this year, but have no other travel plans at the moment.

Christabel Cumberlege (Jacques) Two big happenings for our family. Alice arrived last October to join her two elder brothers Rupert and Ralph, and we are so delighted to have a granddaughter. Second bit, Mike and I met each other exactly 50 years ago today, 5th March, and married 6 months later on 11th September. This year we will be celebrating on the River Douro, which I am told is Portuguese for gold. That and a family gathering the week before in a very comfortable hotel in South Devon should be fun, South Devon weather permitting.

Rowena Ginns (Cullin) Bill is still President of The Coaching Club, so life revolves around the various meets, Newport in Rhode Island being the main one this year, and the usual ten days at Royal Ascot, all very enjoyable with ten American friends coming over. Son James still in Hong Kong, but now has an apartment in Cambridge, which is convenient for the boys at Oundle. Jonathan is based in the New Forest, but abroad much of the time, so don't see too much of them all. I meet **Sue Hicks (Harker)** quite often for lunch, which is enjoyable.

Jenny Hayward (Williams): Bob and I go alternately to Cyprus every couple of months as we have adopted two more stray dogs there. However we have decided it would be best to bring them back here to prevent all this to-ing and fro-ing and being apart so much, so by the end of the year hope to have them back here with the other four. I only hope they will get on! This summer we are going to Connemara again, with 2 of the dogs. Then we are going to Barcelona by train, to stay with a former student. During this time, my regular house and pet sitter Brenda will be here.

I had an operation (full hysterectomy you can't see a mark!) last March for endometrial cancer, which was swiftly diagnosed and dealt with (hurray for the NHS). I have check-ups every few months and all seems well. I hear regularly from **Penny Porter (Nicholson)** in Australia, **Patricia Hegarty (Ballard)**, **Ros Clarke (Langley)** and **Ann Williamson**. I hope we'll all be around to meet up in 2017 for our 60th anniversary at WB!

Alison Reed (Hill) We continue to enjoy our trips to Northumberland. Sadly, Anthony is not too mobile these days, but he manages, and has the interest of his horses and keeps in touch with the gallery world.

Last week I did the first stage of the Thames Path, starting off at the Source and getting as far as Cricklade, sadly a bit early to see the fritillaries. I am doing this with a group - rather too large - but at least we have the benefit of a coach at either end for transport. Having missed out on the Highgrove trip last year, I am hoping to be successful in May. I much enjoyed the School's Christmas Carol Service in London last December, and it is good that it is to happen again this year.

I have also enjoyed meeting up with several Westonbirt friends in the past year. **Maddy Williamson (Langford)** and I had lunch in Oxford with **Charlotte Taylor** in the autumn (a birthday celebration), and in January **Fiona Love (Holland)** and I met up at **Rachel Phillips (Palmer)**'s most attractive mews house in Holland Park. Living on four floors as we do, I felt rather envious. **Margaret Blackburn (Taylor)** and **Angela Potter (Tracy)** bob up from time to time. It is one of the many nice things about London that one can see friends very easily, and there is always so much going on.

Angela Potter (Tracy) After a very busy start to 2014, we continued to celebrate our Golden Wedding anniversary by revisiting Assisi, where we had gone on our honeymoon. Perhaps it was the rose-tinted spectacles, or more likely the fabulous Calendimaggio, but it was a wonderful trip, and one we would happily repeat. We travel whenever we can, whilst trying to ensure control of the jungle that would be our garden if we abandon it for too long. Next stop Amsterdam, then France and possibly Georgia.

Meanwhile I have my London charity, the Friends of the Rose Bowl, which supports a local youth club, and my involvement with the Holfords of Westonbirt Trust, for whom I guide visitors round the state rooms of Westonbirt House. The idea is to raise enough profile to enable a successful lottery grant towards restoring the garden and the interior. The silk-covered walls of the Reading Room and the Dining Room are in a particularly bad state, as is the external stonework in the garden, and there is much else needed to be done. I've become quite an expert on Holford history – something I would never have anticipated! Never a dull moment, with ten grandchildren (aged 4–18) to fill any spare time. We've just returned from skiing with two of them!

Ann Williamson I had a very enjoyable and interesting visit, with a friend, to Petra and Jordan last spring. As I have been a member of the Scoliosis Research Society for many years, and support it, I have had treatments down in Harrow. The consultant covers my age group, and Scoliosis people from 70–80 years are treated by him from all over the UK. Since December I have had a lot of investigations for other issues, so health life has been hectic!! I keep up with **Susie Brookes (Shaw)** and **Jenny Hayward (Williams)**. I am still playing some golf!

Section 26 (1956)
Section Representative:
Angela Potter (Tracy)

Again I start with sad news. **Valerie Sill (Marsland)**'s beloved husband Jonathan died very suddenly in February. I'm sure that those of us who have not already done so send her our sympathy. She writes that everyone has been so supportive, and that she has heard from **Liz Blood (Plant)** and **Sallie Dinham (Abrahams)**. She and Jonathan had a good year spending most of the lovely summer of 2014 at their Devon property, enjoying the constant view of the ocean.

Felicity Coultard (Scott) Following the floods of May 2013, we were in rented accommodation for over a year, while our home was completely waterproofed. All our worldly goods were moved several times, and we are still looking for some of them. It is good to be back, and we have gained underfloor central heating among other advantages. Otherwise little to report, the eight grandchildren are growing up and all well, here, in Edinburgh and in the Falkland Islands.

Sandy Elkington (Johnson) I managed to fit in two great trips this year, in addition to my busy home life of bridge and the Social Committee for the local church. The first one was last June when we flew to San Francisco before picking up a car, heading for the National Parks and ending up with some old friends in Houston, Texas, covering 4,000 miles in all. The scenery was certainly spectacular and well worth the miles we covered, which I have to admit is very easy to do in the States. The second trip was a cruise around South America starting in Valparaiso, Chile, and ending up in Buenos Aires. Not really into cruising but it was the easy way to do it, and my husband was very keen to go round Cape Horn. He was very disappointed that the sea was as flat as a pancake!

The family is flourishing, fortunately, and we are just hoping our eldest grandson, Thomas, who lives in Madrid, will get the grades for a place at Leeds University to read Environmental Science next year. It is certainly a bit closer! He had an amazing experience last summer teaching English to some Buddhist monks at a monastery in the Himalayas, which should look good on his CV. Tom and I are lucky to be so well, and long may it continue! We seem to cover great distances around the world but never seem to manage Gloucestershire!

Jane Hancock (Quale) We have had a traumatic couple of months. David and I were on a Swan Hellenic cruise off Japan when we heard our youngest grand daughter (aged 10 months) had been rushed to Great Ormond Street hospital with a brain tumour. This was removed by a wonderful surgeon, but was found to be very malignant so the poor little girl is currently undergoing chemotherapy with its resulting sickness etc. We are spending some time down in St Albans where the family are currently living so as to be able to help look after their two year old as well as give support. Our elder daughter who is normally in New Zealand had come over for Christmas and has stayed in St Albans to help for the time being.

During the last year we did go on several cruises, which were very good. Unfortunately the one to the Black Sea was after the Ukraine crisis started so was very different to what we had booked but enjoyable all the same. Our other daughter's three girls are growing up! The eldest hopefully will graduate from Durham this summer. The next one is in her first year at Oxford and the youngest is doing GCSE this summer.

Cyrilla Potter (Monk) Roy (who is seriously handicapped) and I had a few days at Whatley Manor, near Easton Grey; this brought back memories of time at WB.

We enjoyed a holiday in the summer in Dorchester, with my 21-year-old grandson. We were told that the hotel was wheelchair and disabled accessible. On arrival they had to remove a door to enable us to enter our room. The bathroom was totally inaccessible to a wheelchair, and the only place to park it at night blocked our exit door. I was taking clean towel deliveries through the window! Otherwise we had a lovely time. But if anyone knows of a hotel with facilities for disabled people within an hour's drive of Salisbury, please let me know.

Unfortunately I had a fall while going to buy the Sunday newspaper ten weeks ago, and have not been able to get out of the house except for a dear friend's funeral at which I gave a tribute. The lovely lady priest helped me up to the lectern and back. My daughter, who lived almost next door for the past eight years, has left her teaching job and gone to work in Colchester. The day she left was a very sad time for me. I sorely miss her. My grandson Alistair is loving life in London at the Royal College of Music. He is currently composing music for a film. My granddaughter Bryony is going to work in China for three months.

I was so sorry to hear that **Mags Alexander** has died. I knew her well and used to go out with her parents. Also, what a shock to hear about **Paddy Angus**'s death; we used to love going over to her home. Her lovely mother made gorgeous meringues for us. I suppose none of us feel old, therefore are surprised when our friends die. Has anyone any news of **Wendy Stewart**?

Anne Renard (Matthews) 2014 was not the best of years, as I had to have my knee replacement redone because of a fracture, then six weeks in plaster to make sure it was mended. Then had to contend with double vision, a symptom of my Parkinson's, but thanks to some excellent opticians, now under control with special prisms in my glasses, and I can drive again. Did manage with help to keep the garden looking lovely and giving me a real boost.

We had a really enjoyable trip to Seattle in July to stay with daughter Caroline and Andrew. Hope to go again this year. I keep in touch with **Liz Wicks** and **Averil English**, and have met **Elizabeth Bennett** through a mutual friend. Sorry for sparse news but best wishes to all.

Oriel Rogers Coltman (Corbett) At last some new news! After a few years of deliberating, we finally decided to move south from Northumberland to Shropshire in 2013. However, it took more than a year to achieve this. We tried to sell Berryburn in the summer of 2013. The land went quickly, but as no one wanted to buy the whole property, we withdrew the house and policies and started again in spring 2014. We eventually found a lovely young family to buy the house, and they moved in in September. We had found our new home earlier that year and moved at the end of August. We are in a village at the bottom of the drive of our daughter, Lucinda and her family. Our elder son Julian lives near Ludlow (25 minutes away), and younger son Simon lives near Much Wenlock (45 minutes away). Between them, they have given us eleven grandchildren. It is wonderful to be near them all and not have to make the 300 mile plus journey from the north to see them. Of course we miss our friends in Northumberland – we had been there for 50 years – but we hope they will come and visit us here.

I miss dear **Sue Powell** so very much. She was one of my oldest friends, and it was so unkind that such a wonderful person should have had her life cut short in such a cruel way.

Section 25 (1955)
Section Representative:
Jill Gibson (Connor)

I am very sorry to report the death of Paddy, **Patricia Scott-Clark (Angus),** who died on 18 October. **Angela Tracy (Potter)** kindly represented me at her funeral service as I couldn't go. She said that the Church was packed with friends who had known Paddy all her life (she had always lived at Uley), as well as her family. We send them all our sympathy.

Elizabeth Abrahams (Langford) I attended the Carol Service at St Dionis, Parsons Green which I greatly enjoyed. The presence of those of my vintage was sadly lacking.

Beth Barrington-Haynes, always a faithful correspondent, writes of her culture filled life: visits to Roussillon and Catalonia, local 'live' Opera in cinema in Holland Park and Ulysses in Ilford. She also enjoyed catching up with **Alyn Denham-Younie** after many years. The farm she has with her brother in Dorset made a profit – hurrah.

Janet Davies (Norman Moses) says that they seem to have been plagued by health issues this past year – not particularly serious but enough to prevent them doing much travelling however they did manage to get to Sardinia in the autumn. She says 'I'm involved with the Botanic Gardens, our local book group and fortnightly walks with friends. A grandson at University in Bristol ensures seeing more of that family, and Skype allows us to maintain contact with the family in Sweden'.

Patricia (Puff) Drew has given up her two-day printmaking workshops, but is still busy exhibiting her work and enjoys the company of other artist friends in Oxford. Puff keeps in touch with many of her year, **Jennifer Grant Renwick** and **Sylvia van Beek-Jackson** to name but two.

Bridget Frost (Kell) still misses Robin dreadfully, but is so grateful for the support of her three grown-up children. She now has to face the clearing out of the family home of so many years prior to moving to a smaller house. Good luck with this, Bridget.

Carol Glazebrook (Wade) says that four grandsons and now two little girls make her take more interest in Westonbirt doings. She would love to be in touch with anyone who remembers her and lives in her area.

Veronica Graham-Brown (Howarth) was getting ready to go for a visit to Florida when she wrote, where she hopes to visit the Everglades National Park. She hitchhiked there in 1958 with school friends with whom she is still in touch. Her family, four children and 10 grandchildren ranging in age from 26 to 9, are all well. She was able to watch her 15-year- old granddaughter in *Grease* this year. It was excellent.

Patricia Hedges (Crowe) is well settled in Cheltenham, and has been able to visit Coulommiers in France for a week and do an opera tour of Italy last year. She is hoping that she and her friend Tony will be allocated tickets for La Scala this year. The Newfoundland puppy they got last year is now 14 months old, and is 16 kilos heavier than Patricia!

He lives with Tony as he doesn't fit into Patricia's apartment! She is still in touch with all of the girls she mentored over the past 25 years who all have their own careers and families now. She is also working for a French exam, which would allow her to study at certain French universities. Good Luck with the studies.

Lynn Levy (Drapkin) We had an interesting trip to China in June - amazing to see how developed the infrastructure of the big cities is. Unfortunately we weren't able to see the country areas. We are loving our new house and see **Liz Abrahams (Langford)** regularly.

Alison Maguire (Mason) is still enjoying living in the Scottish Borders and continues with her everlasting research on Tweed houses. Her sister Julia will be 80 this year.

Jill Gibson (Connor) This past year seems to have been Golden Wedding celebrations for ourselves and many of our friends. Our treat was a safari to Botswana, simple camping in tents in the game reserves, sitting round the camp fire under the stars in the evenings, and seeing so many animals at such close range by day it was incredible. Of course, we also partied!

Liz's cataract was successful so now we are watching her closely to prevent the cataract in the other eye reaching the same size. Everyone is well and grateful to be so.

*(**Barbara Anderson** has been transferred to her correct section, 27, where her news now appears.)*

Section 24 (1954)
Section Representative:
Alison Robinson (De Courcy-Ireland)

Jennifer Andrews (Clair) prefers to stay put at home in Cornwall with her husband Barrie and is still resisting the lure of email as they don't want to be bothered with scams, spam, twitter, facebook, tons of advertising "or other viral nonsense".

Elizabeth Bennett (Anning) celebrated her eightieth birthday party with her whole family gathered together. She writes "My mantra is 'just be thankful for the bits that do work' strengthened by my dentist telling me that I have the jaw joints of a 30 year old!" Elizabeth says she creaks away at Pilates, which she thoroughly recommends, reads, gardens, does jigsaws, goes to a philosophy class at the U3A, at which she modestly says she bats well above her league but "I like to think it keeps what I am pleased to call my brain stimulated". She sees **Anne Renard (Matthews)** with whom she has many a reminiscent laugh over their time at Westonbirt.

Elizabeth Ells (Rawlence) says that she is so fortunate to be living in the same house her husband and she built on the bank of the Ottawa River in 1963 and which they moved into on Christmas Eve, a move encouraged by her sister Emily who was keen to spend Christmas with them in their new house. Circumstances change, but the serenity and beauty of the river is a constant anchor in Elizabeth's life. She remarried some ten years ago, and Tom is still enchanted by living there. As a fanatical cross-country skier, he is not as perturbed by the two months of frigid (frequently -35°C) weather as others are.

Elizabeth writes that her three daughters and six grandchildren all continue to lead busy lives. Louise made a huge mid-life lifestyle switch and is now completing her doctorate on Alice Munro's writing at Anglia Ruskin University in Cambridge. She adds "I recently wrote a slim, illustrated volume of "Letters to my Grandchildren" which included memories of my happy times at Westonbirt. Above all, it illustrates how irrevocably the world has changed since our childhoods."

Sadly, Elizabeth's two younger sisters both suffer from chronic and debilitating illnesses, so she sent in news of them to be forwarded to their relevant sections.

Amelia Gardener (Langford) It's sobering to realise that another 0 is looming, a very big one. Knowing I have outlived some of my school and college friends and acquaintances, and seeing some of the health problems of friends and neighbours, I realise that I have much to be thankful for, that I am still mobile, in good health and have a loving husband who is also fit and active. We have rented a large house on the outskirts of Hereford, my home city, for a family celebration in July, which we are much looking forward to. We were very gratified in February to have a five-day visit from our nearly 16-year-old grandson who came from Yorkshire by train at half-term. But then we do live in a very nice place with fabulous sea views. As a local Fairtrade champion I have been trying to urge churches to sign a pledge that they will only serve Fairtrade coffee and tea etc. So far 65% of churches in Wales have signed, and time is running out to reach the 70% required for the Church in Wales to become the first Fairtrade Province.

Rosemary Kitson (Hines) says she has no news to add to last year's: "Just getting older, like we all are!"

Janet Knight (Sykes) also says she has little news but is hoping to meet up with **Gillian Sandeman (Wright)** while the latter is in UK *(see below)*. Janet has two granddaughters at uni (Durham and York), two grandsons in Australia and three grandchildren at school.She still played tennis last summer, but fears a second hip operation looms.

Sheena Mackenzie wrote that the worst part of her year was the death of **Paddy Scott-Clark (Angus)** with whom she had been friends since her first day at Westonbirt. The better part, earlier in the year, was her grandson getting married in Cuba. She writes: "It was a blast! I suppose it could be a disaster if one faction didn't care for the other, but we all got on very well. This old girl was referred to as the matriarch by cheeky kids and grandchildren, but I suppose it is true somewhat as I looked down the generations present. Another grandson to get married in Jamaica next year, so a repeat performance."

Suzanne Mitchell (Munro Faure) also thinks she doesn't have any interesting news other than getting older and stiffer in the joints. But she then gives an entertaining account of a lovely holiday in central Wales and a completely mad coach trip to Paris with four ladies in the village. "We all had on our bucket list a trip to Monet's garden at Giverny. So off we went in October, longer journey than we were led to believe (Penzance to Paris via Dover/Calais) arrived at the hotel and a complete blackout, eventually found another hotel, arrived at 2.30am next day, no single beds so had to share, fabulous day at the garden, blue skies, masses of flowers, interesting house, in the evening to Montmartre where there was a beer and wine festival (no one told us), absolutely packed, and then some very good fireworks, so could hardly move in the crowd. Next morning should have done a tour of Paris but no one told the driver there was a marathon running, so most roads closed! So off to Fontainbleau, nice day and great French market and a cruise on the Seine in the evening. Left for home next day and finally arrived back in Penzance 20 hours later."

Valerie Moorby (Holmes-Johnson) is still trying to sell the bookshop, so that she can retire, preferably before she hits 80! She had a knee replacement last summer, which limited travelling, but despite now waiting for the second one to be done, hopes to be able to join a small group for a garden holiday booked for May and, if all goes well, do something later in the year as well.

Val still finds it very strange being on her own after so many years, but family and friends make it possible, and she did have a very enjoyable weekend in London with all her girls in December.

"All my family are fine and in various stages of changing jobs and/or houses so we all compare notes. One daughter and I are on a par for the number of times our sale has fallen through!"

Heather Owen (Grange) Moving out, moving in and moving on. I expect many of us will move out of the homes we have occupied in younger days and maybe downsize.

But it is difficult in advance to imagine what an enormous upheaval this entails - not least, what to do with all the things that have accumulated! As both my daughters live in Cornwall, I decided to leave Hampshire, and move down to be near them and the grandchildren. I was lucky to sell my house privately to the daughter of a friend and the whole transaction went through quickly, with no agents involved.

They are a charming young couple, and it is good to know that a much-loved house is now in appreciative hands. I moved temporarily into my daughter's house, nearby, as that was also for sale, and house-sat for six months, whilst commuting to Cornwall, looking for a new cottage. I found one in the village of St Tudy, and have been busy refurbishing and waiting, in another rented cottage, for the builders to finish.

The village community is very friendly, and there is a church, pub and wonderful village shop and post office, but there is still a long way to go, with unpacking boxes, all the change of addresses - not just personal, but utilities, driving licence *et al*. I am finding it an exhausting process but am spurred on by help from many, including encouragement and cards from many OWB's and would welcome any OWB's to visit when passing!

Mary Rusinow (Worthington) I was very sorry to see the deaths of so many people of our era, including my cousin **Joan Freeland (Temple)** and **Juliet Townsend (Smith)** whom I remembered welcoming as a new girl in the summer term. Letitia and I had a bit of a panic discovering what her mother's name was as we could hardly address her as Mrs Smith!

Life continues much as before. but getting old is not funny. However, I keep up my travelling lifestyle. Angus the dog and I spent our usual six months in Italy, and I took off for the last of the enrichment voyages on the student ship, sailing round the Baltic and taking in Poland, Lithuania and Estonia as new countries, before heading off to the Shetlands and Iceland. I would not have gone for so long except that this was the last time. It is a pleasant way to travel.

Christmas was exhausting, first in New York where we were 13 and then in Florida. Alison brought her three to see a little of their second country, and they did New York, skiing in Vermont and then to Florida first with me, and then all of us at Disneyworld.

I was so tired after four days of six grandchildren that I sat down upon my return home and did nothing at all for the rest of the day. No other travels, though I should love to get to Cuba. Possibly South Africa in the autumn, we will see.

Gillian Sandeman (Wright) I am happy to be writing to you from (relatively) balmy Edinburgh – it's 7°C here this afternoon, but at home in Canada it's 22°C with the wind chill. We had a brutal winter last year, and this February it's apparently even worse, so good to be back in Scotland for a few months. We came in mid-January and will leave in mid-June. We're enjoying visits from family and friends, some from Canada and others from England. We are now proud and doting great-grandparents of seven-month-old Lauren, who visits frequently as she lives in Edinburgh. Being a great-granny feels like a natural progression in life; what I'm finding very odd is seeing my baby turned into a granny. That baby and her husband have settled into our home town of Peterborough, Ontario, where our Scottish son-in-law is learning the Canadian winter skills – snow shoeing, cross-country skiing and snow shovelling.

Our younger daughter has moved in the opposite direction. She's left Peterborough and is now settled in Nottingham with her new partner. Our son and his family have remained in Ottawa, although our granddaughter spent her last year of high school white-water kayaking in Peru, Chile, California and Quebec with a tiny peripatetic school called the World Class Academy: no false modesty there! While tackling the waterfalls and rivers, the students also complete their academic requirements. She has spent her gap year on the upper reaches of the Nile in Uganda working at a white-water rafting resort, taking videos and photos as mementoes for the tourists, and in the fall she will be starting a degree in photography in British Columbia.

When at home, I'm continuing to serve on various boards. The most challenging is the board of our community Credit Union: lots to learn. It's good to see the Credit Union movement gaining strength in Britain. My husband, Ian, now in his eighties, is continuing with his research on the calcification mechanisms in the skeletons of corals. This necessitates lots of trips to Jamaica – three last year - as we don't have a lot of reefs in Ontario.

Last July we rented a lovely villa in Puerto Morelos, a village in the Yucatan, and invited the family to join us. Most of the time we were a dozen in the pool and round the barbecue, but for a few days we had all our offspring, two of three of their spouses, and all the grandchildren, which brought the total to 14. It's rare for us to have everyone together.

So many of our generation have children around the world, and, as we age, it feels important to ensure there are opportunities for them to gather. I know they'll come to our funerals, but I want to enjoy their company while I can!

Alison Robinson (De Courcy-Ireland) Getting a 75% response to my request for news makes carrying on as section representative worthwhile, so many thanks to all who replied.

Despite our increasing age (and even more of us will have passed the 80 mark by the time the rest of you read this), in true Westonbirt fashion, we keep as active as age permits, having knees and hips done, moving house, travelling the world, and being grateful for friendships forged all those years ago.

I too am one of the ones anticipating a major birthday later this year! I still continue as a Samaritan listening volunteer, and I enjoy visiting friends (increasingly in residential care, alas), belonging to book and study groups, and keeping up with grandchildren. We had a wonderful Christmas this year: my daughter and family came from Australia, my son and family from Belgium, and the rest of the family from different parts of the UK. We were 22 on Christmas Day and 23 on Boxing Day, when, for about an hour, we managed to get all 13 grandchildren together for the first time ever (youngest wasn't born last time), so we have wonderful photographs and many happy memories.

Like Sheena I was very sad to learn of the death of **Paddy Scott-Clark (Angus)**, particularly as only a few days before she had come in to the AGM specifically to tell us that **Sue Powell (Watson)** had died earlier in the week, so Paddy's own death came as an even greater shock.

Section 23 (1953)
Section representative:
Elizabeth Noyce (Clarke)

Elizabeth Noyce (Clarke) If you didn't reply this year, I hope you will next year. You don't have to send news - it would be good to just hear that people are still keeping well. Just let us know you are there!

Valerie Bell (Duckworth) Apart from getting older and slower I think it might be a relief to take me off your list of contacts as I really do not have any news worth mentioning – other than the mind is not keeping up with the pace of life! *(No Val, it's just good to hear that you're still with us!)* I am so behind with everything in this 'electronic age' and I don't really want to continue pressing buttons.

Jenny Botsford (JJReynolds) My London house seems to have become a mecca for grandchildren at university to invite quite a number of friends to stay. Granny is becoming spot-on at huge breakfasts served very late after they have had a night out. As I am just putting my house on the market and will move to a two bedroom flat down the road in Kensington, I did say that it might not be so easy for them in future. The response was "never mind, Granny, we'll all sleep on the floor!"

I am trying to downsize whilst I can still leap up and downstairs like a mountain goat (sort of). It is a huge job. Some furniture and other things have gone to family. Other things are packed up ready for a table sale in the spring. The idea is to have the house really light, spacious and pristine for the sale. Some things will go to auction when I move. But I am really looking forward to living on a smaller scale, and I will probably go to Mallorca more often.

The year seems to have gone like a flash. I am involved with various things here in Kensington, from managing my son's house, which is let, to being Vice-Chairman of the local Conservatives. I have been to the flat in Mallorca quite a few times, down to Cornwall with the family, several trips to Somerset including a lovely family Christmas there, and the Hong Kong contingent have been over here a lot too. One of the recent excitements was that a researcher funded by my son Chris's charitable foundation *(admcf.org)*, which focuses on both children at risk and the environment, found a new species of frog in Indo-China and named it after him. *Leptolalax botsfordi* is very small and rather ugly, but it is fun to have a family frog!

I see a lot of cousins **Carol Lindsay-Smith** and **Diana Ford** (both **Paxman**) and **Penny Mann (Spurrell)**, and we are in touch with **Laura Marks (Lister)** in Australia. She had a stroke a few years ago and is now living with her son, Adam, near Newcastle, New South Wales. We see her grandchildren when they are over here, and my grandson, William, dropped in on her last summer and had a lovely day with her family.

We are planning a family trip to South America in the summer to celebrate my big birthday. We will fly to Lima and then go on to Machu Pichu, the Amazon Forest and end up in Rio. All hugely exciting!

Gillian Henson (Groome) Another healthy year! I feel lucky – 80 this summer! I'm still living in Tiverton in Devon, and any WB passers-by are always welcome. I've had a bonanza year for travel. I thought I'd better visit friends in Amsterdam, New York, Vancouver and Paris while the going was good! I now have more time to get down to doing my water-colours, and I am showing this year at the Tiverton Art Society Exhibition in March. Tickets are limited!

Helen Lilley (Blakeborough) I moved in October 2013 from Leeds, where I had lived since 1964, and now live far up in the North East at a place called Cramlington. No one except the locals seem to have heard of it! It is actually quite a large town, just off the A1 north of Newcastle on Tyne. My daughter and family live within walking distance, but out of sight(!) That is the primary reason for me moving here. I don't have much news of travels etc, but am very happy up here. One problem though is that it is very cold for most of the year – not much rain but a lot of wind. I am about two miles from the sea, which is a novelty for me. I used to drive down to see my son in Gerrards Cross, but 350 miles is too far these days!

Rosemary Mulholland (Hawkins) How the year has flown by, and we are still jogging along. Last May, Zara joined us: she is a retired Assistance Guide Dog, a beautiful five-year-old golden retriever, so John and I are both kept walking, which is excellent exercise besides having a wonderful friend.

It is hard to believe that John Charles has had his fortieth birthday, and became last year's Man of the Year of Profit, a global company where he is an Innovation Manager of the London branch. James is also based in London, running Redset, his recruitment business. He spent a well-earned and enjoyable Christmas in Spain with his friends. With luck, I am hoping to attend the October reunion this year.

Elizabeth Noyce (Clarke) We have had a rather difficult year! After his stroke at Christmas 2013 my husband was doing well, but came down with a bump after trying to do too much last summer. He thought he could go back to playing in bowls matches and mowing the lawn with a heavy motor mower – he learnt the hard way. Hence he now gets fed up and frustrated because he is unable to do the things that he wants to do. On top of all that, he now has to treat his diabetes with insulin, so we have to take blood sugar readings twice a day – all too much at once! As a result of all this, I have to do most of the driving, here there and everywhere! Not quite as pleasurable as it might be as I have torn the ligaments in my upper right arm, done trying to reach to shut the car boot! It doesn't seem to be too good approaching 80!

Enough of the troubles! We made an enjoyable third visit to Malta last March. Knowing the hotel and some of the regular visitors made it easier. We made three visits to Cornwall, the usual April and October and an extra one in August to attend a wedding that was held in the Eden Project. This was a very pleasant and enjoyable event. This year we are going to Italy instead of Malta for our main holiday – just hope it all works out okay. It's the airports that we find are difficult to cope with!

The grandchildren seem to grow up very quickly. Richard's Natalie (21) is coming to the end of her second year at Southampton University reading Biomedical Sciences. Matthew (18), her brother, takes A levels this summer. Hopes are not too high there. He has suffered throughout his school life with dyslexia and allied difficulties and has lacked help and understanding from the educational establishment. His sister was clever, so why should he be different? seems to be their way of thinking. He is considered lazy. He's a computer guru!

Carrie's son Alex (19) is in his first year at Birmingham University, where he got an unconditional place and then came up with two A*s and a straight A in his A level results! Victoria (16 going on 25) takes her GCSE's this summer. She definitely has a more casual attitude than her brother!

Our dear Cavalier King Charles spaniel, Mr Bingley, is an old man now – 13 at the end of May. He sleeps a lot, but still has lots of puppy energy when awake. He's such a loyal and loving friend to us.

Well, life goes on and we try to enjoy it as much as we can. If only age didn't slow us down so much! Please keep in touch!

Primrose Unwin (Priday) After several years of being left out, Primrose would like to be kept 'in touch'. She says "I often feel inactive but am still battling on!

Section 22 (1952)
Section Representative:
Margot Gill (Wilcox)

Elizabeth Daly Elizabeth has moved into a flat which needs a lot of things altered, and all goes very slowly. Arthritis has taken its toll, results of old falls. Last Christmas she was still in touch with **Kristin Birchenough (Krabbe)** and **Jennifer D'oyley (Jennings).**

Glayne Greenaway (Rocyn Jones) Having recovered from our health problems, my husband and I enjoyed weeks in New Zealand over Christmas and New Year, when we had a wonderful visit to our son and family. The three grandchildren are all at University. We also had our French grandson living with us for five months while he was an exchange student at Bath University.

Lady Henniker (Julia Mason) The year has been very quiet and I have been very well and have made a few small expeditions to see friends and family. We have a lot going on in the village. I now have a great grandson, and the children all seem to be employed or having babies.

Susan Kavanagh (Harris) 2014 was for me the year of the family, and a joyful one it was too. To get us going, youngest daughter, together with her family, arrived in July for a six month visit – the girls, 13 and 15, had a taste of American schooling for one term, and both found this rather relaxing after the rigours of their German high school!

Nathan my second eldest grandchild, serving in the US army, returned from a year's service in Qatar, while Anthony, my third grandchild, returned from Spain, where he had spent one semester focusing on Spanish. A special event was a three-week visit from my sister Rowena, when our days were filled with visits here and there.

Except for Anthony, all the family was present for my 80th birthday celebration and we were all together at Christmas for the first time in eight years. The seven cousins were thrilled to be back together, and for me such a joy to be surrounded by a loving family.

This past year I have seen **Mary Hall (Sercombe)** several times. She has really persevered with her health problems and is probably better now than she has been in a long time. Her youngest granddaughter, Amanda, was married in November.

Mary Nisbet (Lalonde) Mary's husband, Peter, sent an email saying "sadly Mary suffered a stroke last September. She is now comfortable and being cared for at home by her husband and a team of carers. All our dear children and grandchildren are doing fine, and we see them regularly."

Jane Sutton has had more contacts with the school this year than during previous years. A big thank-you to the organisers of our visit to Highgrove. It was a most enjoyable day. I have a royal fir-cone as a memento! (I was however surprised that one had to pay extra for a roll and butter!)

Some of us will remember our connections with a YMCA club in Bristol. Since those days, I have kept up with Pam, one of their members, and I met her at the Arboretum in early June.

Then we went across to the school, and we bumped into the Chaplain, **Alice Monaghan**. As a result of that encounter, I was invited to speak at the meeting of the Christian Union. Unlike in our day, when we met in the old gym on a Sunday afternoon, they meet in the Reading Room with their lunch on a Monday. It was great to meet members and know that as the CU has come and gone over the years, it is now flourishing again.

In contrast to the beauty, stability and freedom which Westonbirt girls enjoy, I went to a conference in Bethlehem in March 2014. Having got through the dividing wall, it was sad to see the restrictions on the inhabitants of the West Bank, especially in Hebron. As two Palestinians and a Jordanian had recently been shot for no reason, there were riots in the streets of Bethlehem. Stones were being thrown at the IDF and rubber bullets were being shot in reply. Twice Palestinians pulled me into buildings for safety. Pray for peace in the troubled countries of the Middle East.

Margot Gill (Wilcox) Thank you to those of you who sent news. It is very welcome. As for most of us, the aches and pains of advancing years are making life difficult, but we all struggle on. My year went very quickly, with 2015 coming as a surprise. I did manage to go to Worcester for a few days, with my Peke, and we also made it to Stamford to see a 91 year old Shell colleague. We stayed in an old coaching inn and had some very good meals! On the return journey, I visited friends I had not seen since 1963. There was a lot of catching up to be done. Letters are not the same. In November I had a fortnight with friends in Denver, Colorado, with plenty of sunshine!

Otherwise, apart from church and Shell Pensioners, I seem to spend a great deal of time on Bible study with a close friend who taught RE. Keeps the brain active.

Section 21 (1951)

Section Representative:
Margot Gill (Wilcox)

Yvette Cregan (Birchall) I have very little news – just getting older and stiffer. Family are well, fortunately

Fay Massey (Waldren) Her husband died and she is now in the process of moving house. (Our condolences, Fay.)

Ann Parsons (Leighton) Life has changed since last year, as husband Christopher died in March last year *(our condolences, Ann)*. It was a sudden diagnosis of cancer but, with help, I was able to nurse him at home until the end. We had just had a wonderful holiday in Canada with his brother, who lives on Vancouver Island.

The village has been very supportive, and I have been encouraged to take up bridge again. I frequently go with friends to the theatre, cinema and pub lunches. I still remain active in the village art group, but have had to give up tennis. I plan to go on a river cruise from Budapest to Bucharest with a friend. I am still in contact with **Bea Roberts (Gunson)**, and we plan to meet up soon, although I find the roadworks on the M3 a bit daunting.

I went to Cambridge to spend Christmas with my elder son and his family, and then we went on to visit the younger one and his family at Kings Somborne. The Hampshire grandchildren are very grown up now. Charlotte is loving her first job in London, and Hugo is going to Bristol University to read geology after a bit of a gap year touring New Zealand by bus. The Cambridge lot are still at school.

Jonquil Solt (Denham Davies) I am still riding and judging both able-bodied and paralympic dressage, as well donkeys, and am now chairman of our local Senior Wives Fellowship. I cannot remember any national or international committee that I joined of which I have not become chairman – but that is life.

We have not downsized, so I am pretty busy gardening for much of the year. Our only animals are three free-range geese (shut up at night) and chickens. We are looking for a mature Labrador who needs a good home, as our black bitch died of old age recently. We feel we are past puppy days as it would probably outlive us. I get great pleasure from the birds, mainly tits, who visit our peanut cage. They can be seen from my computer!

Section 20 (1950)
Section representative:
Jean Stone (Borritt)

Belinda Blackmore (Eastwood) I have very happy memories of my school days and marvel at the way we were able to live such ordinary lives at school during the wartime years. I still see one or two of my friends, **Sarah Bagshaw (Gilbey)** and **Maryrose King (Baines)**, **Joan Clarke (Edwards)** and **Sally Dolphin (Maurice)** - my cousin and my god daughter who is the daughter of **Jennifer Wilcox (Beaty)**. **Lalage Carrick (Swinburne)** and I exchange Christmas cards too.

My life in retirement has slowed down. I walk every week with a group of friends from the yacht club, but I no longer do the full six miles that they do. At 82, four miles is enough for me! I garden, but find the bending down more difficult. I can still enjoy the theatre at Salisbury or Chichester and can drive there, but tend to go to matinee performances, and I can still holiday. Have booked for a garden cruise on Minerva in the Med this year and hope to do a trip to Sicily. Both my granddaughters (now at university) have been playing lacrosse at Westonbirt, and I have been to watch them once or twice, which brings back happy memories of when I was Games Captain.

Lalage Carrick (Swinburne) My husband died suddenly in October so I am now widowed for the second time. I am still working part-time as Consultant with a local law firm in Corbridge, where I am now living. I moved from Gosforth to a smaller house two years ago and am now nearer to my daughter **Astrid (Sadler),** also an old girl.

Gina King (Maclay) I retired from Northamptonshire County Council last May, having served for 45 years. I am still a school governor of a primary school, which includes a pupil referral unit for excluded pupils, many with mental health problems. Fortunately all my family are well, grandchildren grown up, so I await the next stage - to be a great grandmother!

Dorothy Penny (Robertson) I have no news other than a very enjoyable family holiday in Turkey last year. I still play golf and also play my bassoon in a quintet, but osteoarthritis is proving a problem at the moment.

Meriel Pickett (Sharpe) In May I had a wonderful cruise, up the Rhine and down the Danube to Budapest. I spent the first week enjoying the beautiful scenery and fascinating traffic - and sleeping, which relieved much of the strain and exhaustion of recent years. Ben met me in Budapest, and I spent a happy time in Varsad before flying home. In October, I drove 930 miles in a pretty circuitous route up to Kendal, visiting old friends and cousins I hadn't seen for years, including **Shirley Graham**. Now I'm getting to grips with the garden – long overdue. Kind thoughts to any that remember me.

Section 19 (1949)

Section representative:
Jean Stone (Borritt)

Sarah Abel (Poynor) I am getting progressively slower, more stupid and forgetful, but am continuing to keep myself as busy as I can, doing nothing in particular. My family are very good at keeping in touch with me and have visited me, and I have stayed with them too. I went on a cruise over Christmas and the New Year. I enjoyed watching "Posh People: Inside the Tatler" on BBC 2 in December. It made me feel proud of having been to Westonbirt.

Sarah Beattie (Trollope) I moved in June 2014 into a new block of retirement flats. They are very comfortable, and I can have my dog here. I was fed up with looking after my bungalow, and so were my son and eldest daughter. It is very sociable here which is also pleasant.

Christine Geach (Wilson) I have spent the last four years fighting the developers of a valuable AONB, to no avail of course! Like Tetbury, watch out for a mansion tax on Westonbirt or offers to buy some of the land. Rotten government and greedy developers. Sad to hear of **Barbara Scatchard**'s death, she always looked so unhappy and tired after her fiancé was killed. She was extremely prone to travel sickness. I keep fit and alive (so far). The houses being built opposite me are the infamous rabbit-hutches so loved by HMG. Quite a rant!

Beryl Thorp (Holm) As one gets older, the years seem to pass much more quickly. I still get out as much as I can and belong to the local U3A, where there are several groups in which I am involved. For the last five years, I have been churchwarden but am about to give this up. However, our church was given eight bells last year, and we have 15 people learning to ring, so after 40 years I have started ringing again. I am thoroughly enjoying both the ringing and giving the beginners encouragement. I still enjoy my holidays and have just returned from the Canaries. I plan a few days in the Isle of Wight and a cruise in Provence later in the year. The theatre, concerts (especially in the Symphony Hall, Birmingham) are still on my list.

Angela Tickell (Fayle) It is now 18 months since we downsized from Wiltshire and have settled well in Odiham. It is lovely to have all three young close by, although we try not to be too much of a menace to them! All six grandchildren flourish. Georgina (mother of our two great-grandchildren) still lives in Germany, and Laura is in advertising. Helen is a Year 1 teacher and William a trainee solicitor. All are in London.

Chloe and Iona are still at school. Richard and I continue to totter along. I am very arthritic but thankfully can still drive.

Elizabeth Wells (Burt) Another busy year which ended with my needing a stent, followed the same week by a carotid endarterectomy. Having always been in good health, I make a bad patient! The NHS has done me proud. I took part in the Orbita trial, an interesting experience, which for a period involved five different hospitals covering everything. At the moment, the latest bee in my bonnet is student debt. How can it be right to leave university owing sums which when I left school would have bought a family house?

Sections 17 and 18 (1947-48)
Section representative:
Pauline Jackson (Garrett)

Jennifer Barton My long link with Germany is now sadly broken as **Ruth Von Ledebur (Niemann)** died in June. Ruth had joined us in the sixth form in 1948 as one of a group organised by Bristol University to foster reconciliation after the war. She was a great guide on holidays to places like Berlin, Hannover and Weimar.

I was glad to go to the Westonbirt Carol Service in Fulham and see **Susan Curtis-Bennett** there, in good form. No holidays latterly, weekends at Selsey, when I can – lunch outside in the sun (surprisingly often), a little gardening and some good sea air. I have an iPad which constantly disobeys me. I would welcome a less busy life so I could have more time to practise on it!

Ruth Eskens (Page) Sorry not much news. Failing health is making life more than a little difficult. It is not, however, spoiling memories of many happy days spent at Westonbirt – such a long time ago.

Johanna Merz (Bridges) For me it has been a year of highs and lows. The lowest point came when my only sister **Penny Nairne (Bridges)** died after a long illness. I will miss her greatly, as will her large family and many others. My high point came at the end of October when I published my second book of family history entitled *The Luards of Blyborough Hall*. It is currently selling rather well, particularly in the Lincolnshire area. It is available direct from me, Johanna Merz, or online. My two dogs, a collie and a Jack Russell, are still going strong and will be found most mornings on Wimbledon Common, which helps to keep me fit!

Esme Nicholson (Maitland) Time has come for downsizing, every bit of three miles to central Bicester (not our Ecotown of which we are supposed to be very proud). Easier access to shops instead of one bus a day. Address not yet confirmed, but I hope to keep up car driving. In 1947 (or was it 1946?) we cycled from Westonbirt to the very new Slimbridge Trust. Never been since – I'd love to go, by car, I think!

Primrose Minney As a retired journalist, I live quietly in my village, Lawford, Essex – Constable country. I like gardening, reading, listening to music, visiting friends and keeping in touch. Since leaving the *Sunday Times*, I have not had a computer. I am not writing a novel or a memoir. I don't need to know what everyone is doing every two minutes! I can telephone, and my local library provides fax and internet. I go to church and I think prayer is important. I have a cat, Gemma, who likes water!

Jean Edwards (Wates) My friends continue to get email and put up with my limited IT skills. It is a great way of keeping in touch. I am constantly amazed by my iPad's capabilities. It makes me feel like the girl in the Pony Club with the best pony - all the right gear but can't actually ride for toffee apples, or as they would say now, rubbish at riding!

Hilary Nicholson (Bishop) My family visit regularly and it was good to be together for Christmas. I still sing with a small choir, do church recording with the National Association of Decorative and Fine Arts Society (NADFAS) and enjoy activities with the University of the Third Age (U3A).

Section 16 (1946)
Section Representative:
Jane Reid (Bottomley)

Elizabeth Watson (Allen) I am still painting with subjects from Crete and France, and trying to keep abreast mending the church furnishings. Both granddaughters doing exams this summer. Emily has an unconditional acceptance to read English at Nottingham, which takes the pressure off a bit. Otherwise I am well and enjoying life.

Elizabeth Ross (Brigg)'s death was reported by her son two days after her death on 16 December 2014 after a long illness. He said that her time at Westonbirt was one of the really happy periods of her life; in her later years she talked about it often, and she had had a liking for grand houses ever since her school days!

Section 15 (1945)
Section representative:
Jean Stone (Borritt)

Jean Evans (Roxburgh) *(This news was received too late for inclusion last year.)* Still living in Worcestershire, house and garden both too big, but love it. Part-time gardener also in his 80s! Went to Cape Town by sea and back via St Helena (lovely) and Ascension Island (too rough to land).Two grandsons graduated and two last grandchildren on verge of doing so. *(Jean enclosed some newspaper cuttings about Corsham Court and Bowood and commented on how lucky she felt to have been at both during her time at Westonbirt.)*

June Fulford (Layborn) Absolutely no news of any interest! I now have three great-grandchildren and am still alive – if not exactly kicking! I am still in touch with **Elizabeth Hosegood (Robertson)** and **Pauline Cooper (Nock)**.

Mercia Macdermott (Adshead) I was sad to learn of the death of **Joan Freeland (Temple)**, who was formerly my section representative and who, to my everlasting gratitude, persuaded me to attend a memorial reunion at Westonbirt. I hope there are still old girls who remember me as "Mouse"! I am definitely slowing down, although I still attend a weekly group for French conversation, and I am still President of the Friends of Worthing Museum and Art Gallery. My fourth (and last!) biography of eminent Bulgarians was finally published in 2014 by Manifesto Press. Entitled *Lone Red Poppy*, it describes the life and times of Dimiter Blagoev, who, as a student in St Petersburg in 1883, founded the very first Marxist circle in Russia and who went on to found the Bulgarian Communist Party in 1891.

Constance Ware (Inskip) 2014 was not, for me, without a few hitches, including the shock of waking one day with a very squint mouth, very fortunately soon rectified. However, I am flourishing once more. My sister, **Marta Inskip**, who, had she joined the Association, should probably have been about Section 10, died on 9th May 2014, the eve of her 89th birthday after ten years of distressing vascular dementia. I add this news as I had quite a few kind enquiries from friends of hers at the enjoyable visit back to Bowood in 2013. I am extremely sad to note **Joan Freeland**'s death, promptly noted in the newsletter. It was an unwelcome surprise, as we had kept loosely in touch for over 70 years, and I would certainly have been at her funeral. She looked after our section so well until so recently.

Sections 13-14 (1943-44)

Section representative:
Jean Marr

Felicity Atkinson (Fizzy Sutton) is going on a cruise to Monte Carlo at the end of July. She is looking forward to this. Fizzy has had a bad ankle. She lives alone and now has three great-grandchildren.

Gillian Blum (Gregory) I have very little news of interest. Enjoying my retirement home very much and have a nice apartment and good friends. All being well, will go to my great-granddaughter's wedding next October in Southern Ireland.

Rosemary Campbell (Fraser) I moved into a very small two-bedroom house only two years ago, after 64 years in Wasing Lodge. An awful wrench, but it is in the village, where I know lots of people. A fortnight before Christmas, while with my second son, who is a rector, and his wife, I fell down a stair and upset my back. It is taking weeks to heal, so I can't drive. I am very lucky in that my eldest son is only half an hour away and is so kind driving me when he has time. My daughter married in October, aged nearly 50. She is in London. They hope to move to the Tiverton area in the summer. Otherwise, mentally I am fine, but we are all getting very old!

Mary Capey (Reynolds) is still in her own house. She sees her family regularly. Mary and (Jean) had a good laugh over the phone.

Yvonne Phillips (McIlroy) Sadly her sister **Lorna** has died. Yvonne sees her two sons and her daughters-in-law and her granddaughters, who are all very helpful.

Susan Yealland (Simpson) I regret I have absolutely no news at all. Having bad knees and leading a fairly quiet life.

Jean Traill Now 88 years old, I am living in the house I had built about 20 years ago. I have several grandchildren. I am wondering about returning from Spain to live in Holland. I go to Holland regularly to stay with my two sons, but have quite a few friends here, and I am still painting in acrylic. Also bridge, but I am getting a bit forgetful for that. I shall probably stay where I am as long as I can still drive my car, but it is a bit too isolated and no buses out here. Wonderful sea views and a swimming pool in the garden.

Jean Marr Yes, we are all getting older and having to change our way of life. I am very fortunate to have a nice little flat with my two dogs. Making new friends and getting involved in the church. I enjoy Tai Chi every week. I can no longer drive, so have had to get rid of my car. With so many buses and help from friends, I don't really miss it. Thank you all for sending your news.

Sections 1-12 (1931-42)

Section representatives:
Jean Stone (Sections 1-8)
Pauline Jackson (Section 9)
Rebecca Willows (Sections 10-12)

We have not received any news from these early pupils of Westonbirt this year, but we will always welcome contact from them at any time of year. It is gratifying to read particularly in the older members' news how fondly they remember their time at school, and should any wish to relive their memories with a visit to Westonbirt, they are warmly invited to contact Abbie Cooke, PA to the Headmistress, to arrange a suitable time and date.

And finally... are you decluttering?

To those of you who have made it to this page, and who may be having a clear-out due to downsizing or moving house, here is a plea for you to donate any unwanted old copies of the News, or any school memorabilia, for the archives

Please send any donations to Mrs Bridget Bomford, Archivist, at the School. If in doubt, please phone her first on 01666 880333, to check that what you are offering would be welcomed.

Invitation to
Westonbirt Association Members

Westonbirt School always welcomes alumnae, whether on formal occasions such as Reunion Days, or for informal visits to reminisce about your school days. There's always something new to see, in terms of academic and extra-curricular activities, new buildings and projects to restore the old, and current pupils are always fascinated to meet their predecessors. You are also very welcome to bring your family, even if you have no daughters or granddaughters to follow in your academic footsteps!

In the interests of security, and to make sure we are able to welcome you on your preferred date, please contact Miss Abbie Cooke, PA to the Headmistress, to arrange your visit by calling 01666 880333 or emailing *acooke@westonbirt.org*.

Whether or not you plan to visit the school in person, you may also like to visit our website, which is constantly being updated with school news and photos, as well as a picture gallery from the archives.

How to Contact the
Westonbirt Association

The Westonbirt Association database is kindly managed by the School, and so the School is now your first point of contact for any enquiries regarding the Association. Miss Abbie Cooke, PA to the Headmistress, will be able to direct you to the most appropriate person, according to the nature of your query. She will also be able to provide contact details for your Section Representative, whose personal information is no longer included in the News Magazine for the sake of their privacy.

Incidentally, please don't forget to let Abbie know if your own contact details change, so that we can keep you informed of Association matters and can find you if any of your former classmates are looking for you. If you're a fan of social media, you may also enjoy networking with us on the alumni Facebook page:

www.facebook.com/groups/108986984329/

Abbie works at the school full time, year round, so is generally available during office hours. You may reach her via the main school telephone number, 01666 880333, or by emailing her at *acooke@westonbirt.org*. She is always glad to hear from past pupils.

How to Order Copies
of the Westonbirt Association News

From 2015, to gain efficiencies, save costs, and to take advantage of advances in modern technology, we are changing the way we produce and distribute the Westonbirt Association News.

If you are a regular subscriber, you are welcome to go on receiving your copy as before, despatched by the News Finances and Distribution Officer, Jenny Webb, for as long as your account with her is in sufficient credit.

However, you will also now be able to order the latest edition, and all future editions, online, wherever you live in the world. Your copy will be printed in your local territory and sent at local postage rate. If you do this while your account with Jenny is still in credit, she will refund the balance on request - or if you prefer, you may simply donate the balance to the Westonbirt Association Memorial Bursary Fund.

If you prefer not to order online, you may also be able to order a print copy from your local high street bookshop by providing them with the ISBN number of the latest edition. (For the 2015 edition, the ISBN is 978-0-9930879-3-6.)

If, on the other hand, you are one of the many people who prefer these days to read ebooks, you will shortly be able to order an ebook version, which will be made available via all the mainstream ebook platforms, including Kindle, Kobo and iBooks.

We are confident that this is the best way forward for the long-term interests of the Association, and we hope it will also appeal to the younger generation (and many of the older ones!) who enjoy using digital technology. Please be assured, however, that we will always produce print copies for those who prefer them, and also for our substantial Association News archive.

Westonbirt Association
Memorial Bursary Fund

The Westonbirt Association Memorial Bursary was set up in the late 1940s in memory of the five former Westonbirt pupils who lost their lives during the Second World War while they were members of the Forces, Civil Defence or the Nursing Services.

The aim of the fund is to give a bursary each year to help fund the school fees of girls at the school. The Memorial Bursary is still running today, and each year the Association makes an award from this fund to help towards the sixth form fees of one or more pupils.

To be considered for the Memorial Bursary, girls must be nominated by the school in the spring of their Year 11. Candidates complete an application form and are interviewed by a panel from the Westonbirt Association Committee. The process provides good experience for later job and university applications, and, for the successful candidate, receipt of the award enhances their CV as well as providing welcome financial help. Once awarded, payment is made for both years of the recipient's Sixth Form.

Over the years, we have helped more than 70 pupils in this way. With income levels from investments so low at present, and school fees rising, new donations are always welcome to increase the value of the award.

How to Donate to the Memorial Bursary Fund

Cash donations

Payments may be made by cheque payable to "Westonbirt School" and should be clearly marked for the Westonbirt Association Memorial Bursary Fund.

Online by standing order

Please reference payment in the following format:

Account name: Westonbirt School
Sort code: 200384
Account number: 30951927
Bank: Barclays

Bequests

As the school is a charity, bequests are free from liability to inheritance tax. The following are suitable words to send to your solicitor with a request that the Westonbirt Assocation Memorial Bursary be included in your will:

"I bequeath to Westonbirt School in the county of Gloucestershire the sum of £x, free of duty, to be used for the purposes of the Westonbirt Association Memorial Bursary."

You might also wish to inform the school as follows:

"I intend to make a bequest to the school for the purposes of the Westonbirt Association Memorial Bursary."

GiftAid Declaration for the
Westonbirt Association Memorial Bursary

If you are a UK taxpayer, the school can reclaim tax on any gifts you make, via the Gift Aid scheme, provided you fill in the declaration form below in full and return it with your first gift.

Please treat as Gift Aid donations all qualifying gifts of money made *(please circle as applicable)*: *today / in the past 4 years / in the future*

I enclose a donation of £.......... as a contribution to the Westonbirt Association Memorial Bursary.

I confirm I have paid or will pay an amount of income tax or capital gains tax for each tax year (6 April to 5 April) that is at least equal to the amount of tax that Westonbirt School and all other charities that I donate to will reclaim on my gifts for that tax year. I understand that other taxes such as VAT and council tax do not qualify. I understand the charity will reclaim 25p on every £1 that I give on or after 6 April 2008.

Title_____ Forename _____

Surname_____

Address_____

Postcode_____

Signature_____

Date_____

Please notify Westonbirt School if you want to cancel this declaration OR change your name or home address OR no longer pay sufficient tax on your income and/or capital gains. If you pay income tax at the higher or additional tax rate and want to receive the additional tax relief due to you, you must include all your Gift Aid donations on your self-assessment tax return.

Please send donations and the completed form to:
The Finance Manager, The Bursary, Westonbirt School
Tetbury, Gloucestershire GL8 8QG
Registered Charity Number 311715

We would like to thank Alanbrookes Ltd
for kindly auditing the Association's accounts.

ALANBROOKES LTD
CHARTERED ACCCOUNTAND AND REGISTERED AUDITOR

We aim to bring transformational change to local businesses
and the lives of their owners.
Please call Andrew Fisher for a free exploratory meeting on 01453
889559 or email andrewfisher@alanbrookes.co.uk
www.alanbrookes.co.uk